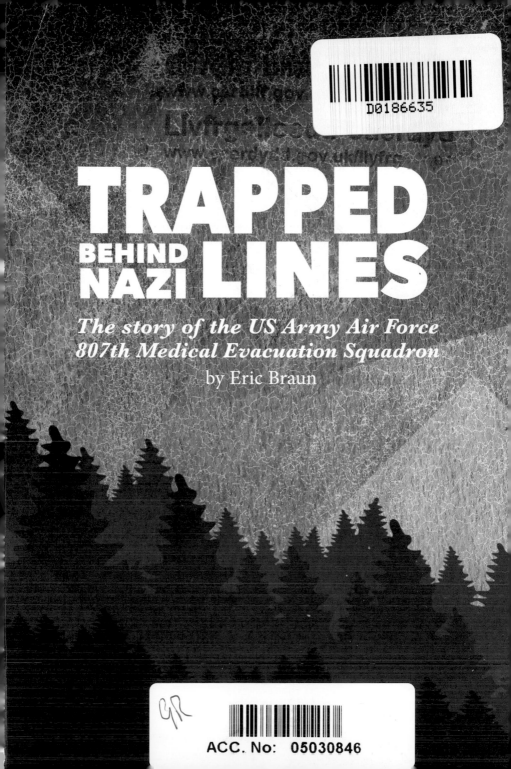

TRAPPED
BEHIND NAZI LINES

*The story of the US Army Air Force
807th Medical Evacuation Squadron*
by Eric Braun

Raintree is an imprint of Capstone Global Library Limited, a company incorporated in England and Wales having its registered office at 264 Banbury Road, Oxford, OX2 7DY – Registered company number: 6695582

www.raintree.co.uk
myorders@raintree.co.uk

Editorial Credits
Mandy Robbins, editor; Heidi Bowler Thompson, designer; Svetlana Zhurkin, media researcher; Gene Bentdahl, production specialist

ISBN 978 1 4747 1063 3
20 19 18 17 16
10 9 8 7 6 5 4 3 2 1

British Library Cataloguing in Publication Data
A full catalogue record for this book is available from the British Library.

Photo Credits
Air Force Historical Research Agency, 212—213, 214, 217 (top); Air Force Medical Service: AFRL Research Division, 215 (top), U.S. Air Force Photo, 215 (bottom), 217 (bottom); Corbis, 208—209; Dreamstime: Nikoini, 26, 68; NARA, 210—211; Shutterstock: Alexander Mazurkevich, 192, andreiuc88, 92, CCat82, 46, ekler, 44—45, Ensuper, 12, Everett Historical, 54, Jiang Hongyan, 152, M. Pellinni, 168, Maxim Petrichuk, 138, nuttakit, 76, Rainer Lesniewski, 108, RossHelen, 182, Sergey Lavrentev, 4, wen mingming, 122
Design Elements: Dreamstime and Shutterstock

The publisher would like to thank Tim Solie, Adjunct Professor of History at Minnesota State University, Mankato, USA, for his help creating this book.

Printed in China.

CONTENTS

CHAPTER 1

THE LUCK OF THE HUNTED

Before the war, when he was back home in Michigan, USA, Orville Abbott was a hunter. He tracked and killed game such as rabbits with expert efficiency. He never thought about how the hunted animals felt. Now, as he ran into the woods, listening for the crack of Nazi gunfire, he felt a jolt of fear run through him. This, he imagined, must be what a rabbit feels just before it is shot dead.

Abbott and 12 other US Army medics and 13 army nurses had crash-landed in Nazi-occupied

Albania almost nine weeks ago. Since then, they had walked hundreds of kilometres in the snow. They had climbed mountains, dodged German soldiers, and ducked under gunfire. They'd hidden in people's homes and in the woods, fought stomach-wrenching illness and malnutrition, and pressed on with gritty determination. Now they were nearly to the Adriatic Sea and a boat that would take them across it to safety in Italy. But in order to reach that boat, they would first have to survive yet another close call.

An American officer, Captain Lloyd Smith, had made his way into Albania to help lead the stranded medical personnel to safety. He was in charge. It was Smith who had somehow got hold of an old Italian truck and a driver so that the Americans could make better time that night. After walking for so many weeks and so many kilometres, sitting in the back of an open flatbed truck – even exposed to the winter air – felt like a luxury. But on the road, they were also exposed to passing vehicles – including Nazi vehicles.

When a Nazi truck approached from the opposite direction, both it and the truck with the Americans stopped. They faced each other in the dark. Smith told the driver of their truck to get out and walk towards the German vehicle. For the medics and nurses, his instruction was to wait. If the Germans turned their headlights on, they should bail out of the truck bed and run into the woods.

THEY'D PROBABLY BE RUNNING FOR THEIR LIVES.

The Americans laid as low and still as they could. The wind moved in the trees along the road and chilled their skin. The idle rumble of the two truck motors was the only sound. Of all the scares they had survived the past nine weeks, this was one of the most intense.

When the driver got a metre away, the German truck turned on its lights, and the entire road lit up with a glare. In a flash, the Americans leapt from the truck and ran as fast as they could for the trees.

Looking back later, Abbott wrote, "I know now how the skin along the back of a rabbit must be crawling as he leaps for cover in those few split seconds before the sting of pellets rips into him and he blacks out with the roar of the hunter's gun behind him."

As they ran, the Americans listened for the eruption of gunfire and hoped they wouldn't be hit. None of them expected to survive this confrontation. But as they dived into the brush and scrambled deep into the woods, nothing happened. Not a single shot was fired.

While their driver talked to the people in the other truck, the Americans waited. The ground was snowy and cold. Because they never expected to spend any time outside of the barracks and hospitals where they worked, none of them had proper winter clothing. For all these weeks, they had been getting by with thin jackets and plain, fraying shoes. Everyone crouched and shivered.

After a few minutes, their driver came back into the glare of the headlights. He found Captain Smith waiting by their truck, and the two of them spoke quietly for a minute. Then the hidden Americans heard Smith laugh.

"All aboard! Come on!" he yelled. "We're getting out of here."

As the nurses and medics climbed back into their truck, Smith explained that the German truck had been stolen by two local Albanians. They were taking it to Allied territory so they could use it against the Nazis. The thieves had thought the Americans were the German patrol.

As the two trucks passed each other and the

Americans continued on through the darkness, a couple

people in the back of the truck began to argue about

luck. It was too dark for Abbott to see who was talking.

A man's voice said that they'd had terrible luck. After all,

they kept running into all these dangerous situations.

Time after time, their lives were in danger.

One of the nurses argued that they'd had terrific luck.

Yes, they had found themselves in many bad situations.

But every time, they had escaped. What better luck

could they ask for?

Soon, they reached a turn-off and got out of the

truck. They carried their measly belongings towards

a farmhouse hidden away from the road. Before they

reached the farmhouse, they saw lights back on the

road and heard the sound of Nazi patrol cars. Once

again, the group hid in the trees and waited while

lights were shined over the woods. Nobody moved.

For a few terrifying seconds, the powerful beam of

light swept over them. It was another test of their luck.

Would it be good or bad? Abbott might have thought

once again about those rabbits. They were terrified of

their hunters. But sometimes the rabbits didn't die.

SOMETIMES THEY ESCAPED.

CHAPTER 2

CRASH LANDING!

Their flight had trouble almost from the start. The plane was bound for Bari, Italy, on a mission to pick up wounded British soldiers. Shortly after the aircraft took off from the airstrip in Sicily, a nasty storm rolled in. Dark clouds filled the sky, and the Mediterranean Sea churned below. Rain pelted the plane, and a heavy fog wrapped it up. The 13 nurses and 13 medics on board the transport began to squirm, but they were careful not to let fear show on their faces. Fear had a way of spreading, and nobody wanted that.

Besides, the 807th Medical Air Evacuation Squadron (MAETS) had flown through storms together before. It might be scary, but they didn't feel their lives were in danger – yet.

One of the nurses, sitting in the front row, was Second Lieutenant Agnes Jensen. She tried to distract herself from the troubling weather by reading a magazine. But it wasn't easy – the plane made sudden drops, climbs and jerks. Horrible cracks echoed through the cabin, and loose equipment flew. Only Jensen's seat belt kept her from flying loose too. She gave up on reading and slipped the magazine beneath her bottom to keep off the chill from the metal seat.

As the aircraft flew higher, the inside got colder. The plane was not insulated, and the hard metal seats were frigid. Suddenly the plane bucked and dived, and it got warmer inside. She looked out her window and saw the sea only a metre below! Were they going to crash? She counted the life vests – there were 10. The plane held 30 people.

Then they climbed again. The radio operator came out of the cockpit to grab some equipment near Jensen and rushed back into the cockpit. The door remained slightly open, and the passengers saw that he was having trouble with the radio. The plane was now flying in circles. Jensen had a bad feeling. Though she and the rest of the squad had flown many missions together, the pilots were new to them. Jensen and the other nurses and medics looked anxiously out of their windows for a sign that they would be at their destination soon. Suddenly Jensen felt a tap on her shoulder. The nurse sitting next to her, Second Lieutenant Elna Schwant, pointed out of the window.

MOUNTAINS.

Where were they? They should have landed in Bari long ago, but there were no mountains near Bari. They must be way off course. How much longer could they fly before they ran out of fuel?

Suddenly the plane banked and slowed. They dropped altitude quickly, and one of the pilots, First Lieutenant Charles Thrasher, came out of the cockpit.

"We can see a field [an airfield] and we're going to try for it," he said. He instructed everyone to buckle up and prepare for a harsh landing. Chunks of ice crumbled off the wings and clanged against the fuselage.

Relieved to be landing at last, the passengers in the cabin chatted with excitement as the plane descended at a sharp angle. They were all eager to be on the ground again. The wheels lowered from the plane. As Jensen peered through the clouds at the airfield, red anti-aircraft tracers suddenly flared past the windows. The glowing bullets tore through the fog, and a few pocked against the plane's wings.

The pilots quickly pulled up and climbed back into the clouds. They banked one way and then another, trying to hide from whoever was shooting. Now Jensen really was worried. Being lost over the Mediterranean with no radio and low fuel was bad enough. Being shot at by artillery was a lot worse. But who was shooting at them?

IT HAD TO BE AXIS FORCES.

• • • • •

The MAETS programme had only been around since December 1942. The Allies developed it to transport wounded and sick soldiers by air from hospitals near the fighting to safer – and better – hospitals away from the front lines. By the end of the war, it was clear that the programme was of critical importance. It had been used to transport more than 1 million troops.

By the night when they took that anti-aircraft fire, the nurses and medics of the 807th MAETS had been together for about six months. They had trained together in Louisville, Kentucky, USA, and shipped out in August 1943. They'd been stationed in Sicily for about a month when they got the call to fly to Bari. Many of the nurses had become friends with one another, and many of the medics had become friends as well. But because the nurses were officers and the medics were enlisted men, the nurses and medics hadn't got to know each other well. They were not allowed to spend time together outside of work.

Twenty-eight-year-old Agnes Jensen was one of the oldest members of the unit and a natural leader. She grew up on a farm in western Michigan in the United States. She had studied nursing in Detroit before joining the army in February 1941. Jensen was looking for adventure. She was assigned to a post at Fort Benning, Georgia, USA. But it didn't take her long to realize that life there wasn't any more exciting than the one she'd left behind. After the Japanese bombed Pearl Harbor on 7 December 1941, and the United States joined the war, Jensen wanted to do more for her country. In early 1943 she volunteered for the MAETS programme. To keep her parents from worrying about her, she didn't tell them about her new assignment. Little did Jensen know just how much adventure she'd find.

On 3 November 1943, British troops launched an attack to capture land near Bari, Italy. Though they took the ridge, they suffered many casualties. The 807th was called in to pick up soldiers on 6 November but fog and rain kept them grounded. The weather remained bad on the 7th, and again the flight was delayed. Meanwhile, men continued to be injured. Help was badly needed.

When finally the weather was deemed clear enough to take off, on the morning of 8 November, the aircraft was assigned a crew of four. Lieutenant Thrasher was the pilot. Thrasher had been promoted to first lieutenant a month earlier and was the highest-ranking officer in the group, despite being only 22 years old. Thrasher grew up in Daytona Beach, Florida, USA. He'd attended Bolles Military Academy in Jacksonville, where he excelled in athletics. He enlisted in the army in 1941.

The co-pilot, Second Lieutenant Jim Baggs, from Savannah, Georgia, USA, spoke with a strong southern accent and liked cracking jokes. Sergeant Dick Lebo from Halifax, Pennsylvania, USA, was the radioman, and their crew chief was Sergeant Willis Shumway of Tempe, Arizona in the United States. This was the first time these four had flown together.

In the last-minute preparations for the flight, the crew had forgotten a few important details. They didn't count the parachutes and life preservers. More importantly, they didn't learn the day's password for air-to-ground radio communication.

When things got difficult, the medics and nurses were careful not to show fear, but the crew in the cockpit grew frantic. The radio wasn't working. When Lebo did get through to Bari, he was refused any guidance because he didn't know the day's password.

As far as the Allies in Bari were concerned, this could have been an Axis plane looking for passage into Allied territory.

To make matters worse, they were having trouble getting accurate readings from the compass – something else they should have tested before take-off.

After the attempted landing on the strange airstrip, two German fighters scrambled to pursue the American aircraft. Thrasher guided the plane to the thickest cloud cover he could find – farther inland. Yet he wasn't sure what country they were flying over.

Luckily, Thrasher was able to lose the fighters. He flew another half hour. The wings were icing, and disturbing bangs came from the spots where they'd been hit by anti-aircraft fire. Thrasher and his crew realized they'd have to make a crash landing. Jensen and others among the unit began to fear that they would die.

Again, Thrasher came out of the cockpit to announce that they were going to try to land in a field in a valley.

Jensen looked out at the icy mountains stabbing into the air and tightened her seat belt. She put her head on her knees and hugged her legs. The crew chief, Shumway, tried to brace himself against a wall – there was no place for him to buckle up.

Thrasher crested a mountaintop and then dived sharply. Orville Abbott, the hunter from Michigan, recalled later that his stomach was turning. He worried that he would pass out. Thrasher eased them down, and everyone felt a jolt as they hit the ground in a lake bed. The terrain was bumpy and harsh, but the aeroplane stayed in one piece. Still, the noise inside the cabin was like an explosion. Their equipment and bags flew forward, hitting the front, as did Shumway.

Jensen tried to lift her head, but the plane's momentum kept it down. Then suddenly the vehicle stopped moving. Its tail reared into the air, and the nose burrowed into the soft earth.

The plane shuddered as the tail fell again to the ground, and Jensen raised her head and looked around. Shumway was in a crumple amid the baggage and medical equipment. Everyone unbuckled and started to stumble out of the plane, thinking an explosion might occur at any moment.

When Jensen reached the exit, she saw that the ground was at an even level with the bottom of the aeroplane's door. When she stepped out, her feet sank in the mud. She looked around. Mountains towered all around them, but they sat in a wide valley. The field was stubbled with old corn plants. It was raining.

A couple of people grabbed Shumway. They set him against the plane, and the nurses began to give him first aid. The crew chief had cuts and bruises on his neck and face, and a big cut on his knee. The nurses cleaned him up, bandaged his cuts and gave him a shot of morphine for the pain.

That's when they noticed some people coming down the mountain and running towards them. Jensen and the others watched the men, not sure what to do. As they got closer, Jensen noticed they were carrying rifles on their backs.

CHAPTER 3

YOU'RE IN ALBANIA

One of the medics went back to the plane to retrieve the Thompson machine gun, the one weapon they had with them. But then Thrasher thought better of the idea. If they held the gun, they'd only increase the chance that a fight would erupt. And they were not likely to fare well in a fight. Instead, Thrasher had everyone wave white handkerchiefs in the air, meaning "we surrender".

One of the strangers to reach the group rode a large white horse and wore a black cape, which flapped behind him. Two bandoliers of bullets slashed across his chest, and hand grenades hung from his waist. A rifle was strapped to his back. To the Americans' relief, he was smiling widely.

"Americano! Americano!" he yelled as he dismounted his horse. He grabbed Jensen's hand and shook it.

"Where are we?" she asked. "Italy?" She pointed to him. "Italiano?"

The man shook his head. "No, no! Russia. Russia," he replied, pointing to the red star on his hat.

Russia? Jensen couldn't believe it. It seemed impossible that they could have flown all the way to Russia.

As the man shook hands with other nurses and medics, Jensen counted heads. All of them were present. They'd all survived the crash. She felt a wave of relief.

As the rest of the strangers reached the plane, rain began to fall harder. One of the men on horseback was the commandant, or leader. He had a thick moustache and long black cape like most of them. He spoke enough English for the two groups to communicate. When asked where they were, he told them – Albania.

That made more sense than Russia, but the Americans felt their spirits drop. If they were in Albania, that meant they'd flown all the way across the Adriatic Sea. It also meant they were in enemy territory, because Albania was controlled by the Axis forces. They were in great danger. About a year earlier, Adolf Hitler had issued his Commando Order. It stated that any Allied soldiers caught behind enemy lines were to be executed.

Getting to safety wouldn't be easy. Albania was a small, rugged country a bit bigger than Wales. It was very poor and lacked good roads. The main modes of transportation were horses and mules. Most of the villages and towns lacked electricity. The Americans knew that Italy lay west across the Adriatic Sea, but they did not know how far they were from the coast. When and if they did get to the coast, they'd still have to find a way to cross the sea. Would someone send a boat? Did anyone on the Allied side of the war have any clue what had happened to them?

• • • • •

The commandant's name was Hasan Gina. He had a strong accent, but his English was passable. Hasan gestured with his hand in a circle around them. "The Germans are all around!" he said. But he told them not to worry. "The Germans do not take you from us."

Hasan and his men were anti-Nazi guerilla fighters.
They wore uniforms of mixed types, including Italian
and German. The Americans assumed the uniforms
had been taken off dead soldiers.

Hasan explained that they needed to get moving
quickly. The Germans had probably seen the crash,
and they could be coming at any time. The Americans
weren't sure they could trust Hasan, but their options
seemed limited. They gathered supplies from inside the
plane. They built a stretcher for the injured crew chief,
Shumway, out of seats removed from the plane. One of
the men set off an explosion in the plane that destroyed
classified equipment that sent coded signals. Then the
bewildered group began trudging after the guerillas
through the woods up the muddy, slippery mountain.
Rain continued to pelt them. It wasn't long before
everyone was wet and muddy.

Within a few hours they arrived at a two-storey stone hut. It was the only building in the village of Gjolen. Several male and female residents welcomed the Americans, who were grateful to get out of the rain and rest. A flight of stairs led up to the second floor of the house. Some of the medics carried Shumway on his stretcher up the stairs to the landing.

A fire burned in a small rectangular fireplace, and on each side of the fireplace was a shuttered window. There was no chimney, and the smoke moved up the wall, which was blackened to the ceiling with soot. There was no furniture, but instead just a few strips of old carpet on the floor. It was smoky but warm, and everyone took turns standing by the fire to try to dry their clothes. The evening had begun to get dark, and the fire flicked their shadows along the walls.

Several nurses checked Shumway's injuries, as well as

a deep gash on Lois Watson's face. They guessed it was caused by Shumway's foot as he flew past her during the crash. The nurses and medics got to know Thrasher, Baggs, Shumway and Lebo, whom they'd just met that day. Then they talked about what their next move should be. The decision was made to hike to the coast and try to get a boat there.

Orville Abbott sat near the flight crew. He listened as Hasan tried to convince Baggs, the pilot, to destroy his aeroplane. Baggs was against it. He appealed to Thrasher, "Are we going to let them burn our ship?"

"She's no good to us, Jim," Thrasher replied. If the Germans found the plane, he explained, they'd kill people in the village to get information about the Americans. "If it's nothing but a charred heap, why, we crashed and burned and that's all they know."

"Okay," Baggs said quietly.

Meanwhile, the Americans were very hungry. They hadn't eaten since the morning. Hasan brought them a tray of flat cornbread, which they ate gratefully even though it was dry and unappetizing. He also brought a few small chunks of sour white cheese that was equally as distasteful as the cornbread. While they ate, a young boy played for them on a kaval – a sort of flute.

It wasn't much of a meal, but as Abbott chewed his couple of mouthfuls, he realized that for these people, who were very poor, feeding the Americans was not easy. This meal was a delicacy to them, served as a special honour for the guests.

Everyone went to sleep in the small room, worried, cold and uncomfortable. Because it was so crowded with all 30 of them in there, several people sat up against the walls. Some of the nurses gave up the liners to their field coats for the medics to use as blankets, since the men's rain jackets didn't provide much warmth. The flight crew members were more comfortable in their heavy flight jackets.

Abbott found a spot near the door, where it was colder but less smoky. He sat with his back against the wall and looked at the silhouettes of his comrades in between short bouts of sleep. He remembered waking up that morning in his bed at the base in Sicily. He remembered eating a hearty breakfast – and he thought about how dramatically his fortune had changed. He was just a young man – 23 years old. He was a long, long way from his home in western Michigan, USA.

"You awake, Orville?"

It was medic John Wolf. Abbott grunted that he was awake.

"I've been thinking," Wolf said. "This ought to be good rabbit country." Wolf was from Wisconsin and like

Abbott enjoyed hunting wild game.

"Nuts," Abbott said grumpily. "There isn't anything in this lousy country."

· · · · ·

In the morning, the Americans took turns using the bathroom – a hole in the floor behind a partition in the corner. Afterwards, they stepped outside to find that their bags had been rummaged through and many things stolen, including scissors, soap, socks and underwear. They asked Hasan about it, but he said only that Albanians never steal. They decided not to push the issue any further. It was obvious from the state of the village that people here were in dire need. They probably needed the stolen items more than the Americans did. Instead, they told Hasan about their plan to hike to the sea and find a boat. Hasan told them that it would be about a two-week hike to the port of Vlorë. He would help them, but first he wanted to check with his commandant in the next village, so he sent a messenger.

While the messenger was gone, Abbott went with Thrasher, Baggs, Lebo and a few other medics back down the mountain to destroy the plane. Hasan sent a scout ahead of them to make sure no German soldiers were around. Now that the rain had stopped, the walk down took only an hour.

At the plane, the men took anything they thought might be helpful on their journey. They took first aid kits, a blanket, a tarp and rations. Abbott took D rations, emergency food made into chocolate bars. They cut up a parachute to use as ropes and scarves. Then they opened the fuel tank in the wing and let the fuel drain out. They filled a container with the fuel and dumped it in the cockpit. Baggs stood in the doorway and struck a match, and the fumes in the air immediately exploded. He flew back into the mud but wasn't hurt. But the fire didn't catch. The men couldn't get the plane to burn. They gave up and went back to the village.

When they returned later that night, they added wood and more fuel to the plane, and finally they managed to ignite it. Abbott watched in silence as oily, black smoke streamed upwards into the sky. To Abbott, seeing the plane burn made their predicament seem more real. They were definitely stranded. What would happen to them?

Abbott had many worries and questions. But one thing was for certain – no enemy would find anything of value in that aeroplane now.

· · · · ·

The next morning, Hasan's commandant arrived in the village on horseback with several men walking alongside him. Hasan, along with Thrasher and Baggs, went out to talk with the leader, whose name was Kahreman. The man spoke no English, so with Hasan translating, they discussed options for getting the Americans to safety. They finally agreed that Hasan would escort them to a village called Berat, which was currently controlled by the partisans. There, they would get assistance from British officers, who would help them make their way to the sea.

But tonight, Hasan announced, they would have a feast. Three men tied a water buffalo to a tree in the yard and slit its throat. Many of the Americans turned away in disgust, but others watched as the animal was butchered and cleaned for the stew. The meat had to feed the village for several days, though, so the Americans didn't eat as much as they might have liked. There were no bowls or utensils other than the big stew pot and one wooden spoon. To eat, they all took turns spooning out a few mouthfuls before passing the spoon onto the next person.

The next day, Hasan and his men led the Americans back into the woods. The forest was colourful, beautiful and peaceful. But the group was careful to watch for signs of the Germans. If they were caught, they'd be killed. One afternoon while they were walking, one of Hasan's scouts came running to report that Germans were in the area. The Americans walked as silently as possible along the path, and although they heard gunfire, they never saw any Germans.

After a few days of hiking by day and sleeping in villages at night, they reached a valley. Berat was on the other side of the valley, which meant they had to cross it. But they'd have to pass the end of a runway on a German airfield as they did. Hasan assured them that if they saw two or three Germans, he and his men would kill them. If they saw more Germans than that, Hasan said, "I am sorry."

Just as they were about to make the crossing, they heard the roar of aeroplane engines. Looking up, they saw six American B-25 bombers fly overhead. The Americans ran onto the field to wave parachutes and hats at the planes. Abbott was so happy to see American planes that tears ran down his cheeks. Moments later they heard the sound of bombs exploding.

Three German fighter planes had taken off from the airfield to chase the bombers, and the Americans crossed the valley while they were gone. But just as the group was nearly to safety, the fighters suddenly banked and returned to land. The Americans hid, and the Germans landed without seeing them. There was no sign that the American planes had seen them either, though they all hoped that they had. It was a difficult moral defeat for the stranded Americans.

In his disappointment, Abbott thought about the telegrams that the army would be sending to their families informing them that their children had gone missing in action. His heart sank as he pictured his mother sitting in their house with the telegram in her hand, a picture of himself at her side. There was only one situation that would have been worse for Abbott's mother, and he was determined not to let it become a reality. He put all negative thoughts out of his mind and, like the others, kept on walking. That afternoon, the group reached Berat.

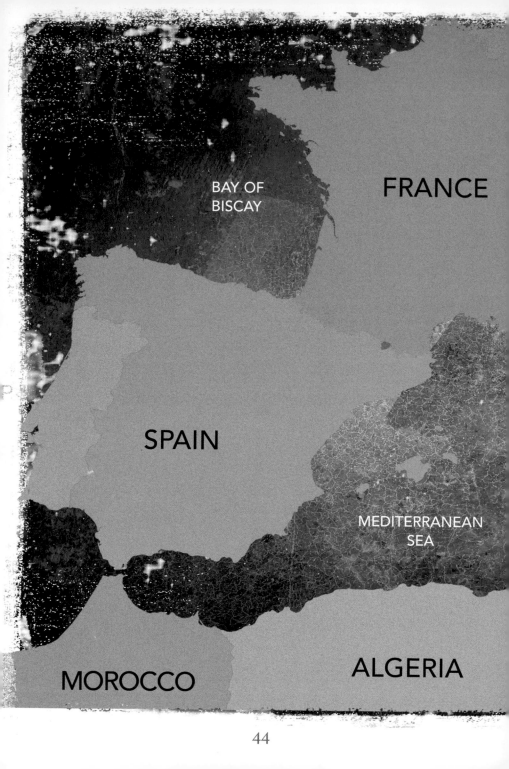

BAY OF
BISCAY

FRANCE

SPAIN

MEDITERRANEAN
SEA

MOROCCO

ALGERIA

GERMANY   CZECH REPUBLIC   SLOVAKIA

AUSTRIA   HUNGARY

SWITZ.

SLOVENIA

CROATIA

BOSNIA AND
HERZEGOVINA   SERBIA

ITALY   ADRIATIC
SEA

ALB.

SICILY

This map shows the intended route of the 807th
MAETS' plane in white and the actual route in red.

TUNISIA

CHAPTER 4

UNLIKELY HEROES

The 807th MAETS was greeted like a band of

heroes in Berat. As they walked down the cobblestone

street, people came out of their homes to meet them,

sing songs and toss flowers to the Americans. Some of

the locals tried to hug them. Some even had cameras

and snapped photos of them. It made the group

nervous because these people clearly expected them.

It seemed like everyone knew they were here. Did the

Germans know too? And why were they being given a

hero's welcome?

The bedraggled group made their way down the main street as if on parade, the residents cheering, "Americano! Americano!" They sang the Albanian national anthem, and then the American anthem, "Star Spangled Banner".

Berat was much bigger than the villages they'd stopped in so far – with about 10,000 residents – and more impressive. It was walled in and featured a castle several hundred years old as well as hundreds of homes. Most of the buildings were one or two storeys and made of white stone.

The group was led to a hall to hear city officials give speeches. An imposing man with abundant dark hair and a moustache translated for them. From what he said they realized that the locals believed they were troops coming to help them fight the Nazis. Jensen looked around her at the other Americans. They were unarmed, hungry, exhausted and totally unfit for battle.

It was almost funny – the nurses and medics were so run down and ill-equipped. How could anyone mistake them for fighters?

Still, the people in Berat celebrated the arrival of the Americans. Doing so was dangerous for them. If the Germans caught them aiding the Americans in any way, they'd be killed. Their villages and towns would be burned down.

Hasan and his men and the people in Berat and all the villages they had travelled through were partisans – friends of the Allies in the war. They were led by Enver Hoxha, the First Secretary of the Communist Party in Albania. He had united the partisan factions as the Albanian National Liberation Army. They received some military support from the British intelligence organization, the Special Operations Executive (SOE).

Hasan himself had killed many Nazis. That, he claimed, is how he earned the leadership of his brigade. If someone else killed more, then that person would become the commandant. As he told the Americans stories of his kills, they grew to respect and fear him.

After the speeches, the group was led to the Grand Hotel Kolumbo for a banquet in their honour. The meal was quite a welcome change from the meals they'd got used to the past few days. Waiters served them mutton, rice, potatoes and cornbread, which seemed to be an Albanian staple, topped off with one apple for each of them. It would have been a humble meal back home in America. But it felt like a feast after the last few days. Certainly the Albanians saw it as a feast as well.

· · · · ·

After dinner, the Americans met the man who had translated the speeches for them, Kostig Steffa. Steffa was tall and wore Western clothes. He spoke many languages, including Albanian, English, Italian, Greek and even some German. He told them he would be taking over for Hasan in leading the Americans to safety. He said that, contrary to what the Americans had been told, there were no British agents in Berat. However, there were British in Albania, agents of the SOE who were helping the partisans, and Steffa could get a message to them. The group would just have to stay in Berat for a couple of days.

They were separated into groups of two or three and placed in the homes of various locals to wait for further direction. While they waited, they were treated to more parades, endless speeches and hearty meals.

Though the unit had trained together for months, many of the men and women didn't know one another very well. Men and women hadn't been allowed to socialize together, and none of the nurses or medics had met the flight crew. During these days in Berat, with nothing but worry and time on their hands, they got to know one another.

Over the next few days, Jensen, Abbott and the other members of the group continued to be paraded around the town. They met many partisans, learned the partisan salute, watched a play and sat through more speeches. They were eager to leave, but there wasn't much they could do. They waited for Steffa to say when it was time to go. While they waited, both Agnes Jensen and Orville Abbott began to take notes on their adventure. Both would eventually turn their notes into books.

As the waiting stretched on, the Americans grew more and more nervous. They weren't sure they could trust Steffa, and they didn't like the fact that locals were posting photos they'd taken of the Americans in town. It seemed risky. On top of that, many of them had severe diarrhoea, probably from food poisoning or unsanitary eating conditions.

Every night, the Americans were put up in different homes or hotels – always in groups of two or three. They didn't realize that being separated could be dangerous for them, but in time it would cause a major problem.

CHAPTER 5

NAZI ATTACK

Early on their fourth morning in Berat, Agnes Jensen awoke to the sound of gunfire. She'd often heard random bursts of gunfire, but it was only partisans shooting off rounds for fun. When louder booms exploded in the area, Jensen knew this was something more serious. It sounded like artillery or tanks.

Jensen was staying in a house with Ann Kopsco, a nurse from Louisiana, USA. On hearing the explosions, the women jumped out of bed, dressed quickly and ran outside. The family they were staying with peered out of the window and prayed. The streets were chaotic. Militia members ran towards the explosions with rifles. Families loaded vehicles with their possessions in preparation to flee the town. Children wailed and cried, and their mothers carried them or pulled them by the hand.

Medics Orville Abbott and John Wolf climbed out of bed slowly at first, then more quickly as they realized something was wrong. The host of the home where they'd slept didn't speak English very well, but they understood what he was yelling at them:

THE NAZIS WERE ATTACKING.

In another house, Harold Hayes and Bob Owen had heard the gunfire. The teenage son of the homeowner scouted the streets and came back to talk with his father in Albanian. Then the father turned to the medics. "It is not good," he said. "Get your clothes on."

THE GERMANS WERE ALREADY IN THE CITY.

As Abbott and Wolf ran into the street to look for the rest of their group, they heard warplanes flying overhead. They caught up with another medic, Charles Zeiber, and they ran towards the hotel. Zeiber yelled something to Abbott about wanting to help the partisans in their fight against the German invaders, a thought that had crossed Abbott's mind too. It must have felt wrong to be hailed as heroes but flee as soon as things got dangerous, leaving the locals to fend for themselves.

But flee they did, and soon Abbott saw Thrasher and the co-pilot Baggs, who were yelling and gesturing towards three trucks that had just pulled up in front of the hotel. Shumway, who was still hurt from the crash-landing, limped his way into one of the trucks. Kostig Steffa directed all the Americans to get in.

Abbott and the other medics climbed into one of the trucks and saw Hayes there. But had everyone made it?

The trucks pulled into the street and began to drive.

Jensen was running through the street with her bunkmate, Kopsco, when Thrasher reached out from a passing truck, grabbed her and pulled her in. As he grabbed Kopsco, Jensen looked ahead to another truck filled with people. She saw several of the other Americans in a truck with Steffa, but it was impossible to tell if everyone was accounted for.

People in the streets were screaming and running for their lives. Amid the chaos, the trucks had to stop. The Americans then noticed that the pedestrians were pointing to German Stuka dive-bombers in the sky. They quickly abandoned the trucks and ran for cover in the woods. Not wanting to be anywhere near machine gun fire, Abbott ran as fast as he could deep into the woods. Instead of firing on the caravan, the planes flew past them and bombed the city. From where he was hidden, Abbott could see a partisan machine gun firing from an old burned-out hospital building in Berat, but the planes were out of its reach.

The Americans lay in hiding for a few minutes before coming out. They boarded the trucks again and drove for only a short distance before the planes returned, and everyone jumped out again. This time the Germans strafed the trucks repeatedly with machine gun fire. Everyone stayed hidden the best he or she could, but the injured crew chief, Shumway, only made it a metre from the road. He was terrifyingly close to the road as the planes passed by four times, pumping hundreds of bullets into the vehicles. By sheer luck, Shumway was not hit. Finally the planes left. The vehicles were riddled with bullet holes and useless now.

By this time, the Americans were hopelessly scattered in the forest outside the city and unsure how to find one another. Hayes and Owen followed the river away from the town until they ran into Jensen, Kopsco, the pilots and a few others from their group. With them was a 23-year-old partisan they'd met in Berat named Qani Siqeca, which the Americans mispronounced "Johnny". Johnny spoke some English.

Checking the road again through Johnny's binoculars, they saw a tank crawling up the road towards them. Behind it were other German trucks and tanks, so the group took cover behind the riverbank. The Germans sat on the road for more than 10 minutes, and nothing happened. Nobody even came out of the hatch on top of the tank. When finally the Nazi vehicles cleared out, the Americans, led by Johnny, began to hike up the mountain, hoping to find safety – and the other Americans from their group.

They hiked as quietly as they could until they reached a small village. They hoped they might see the other Americans there, or hear of them passing through, but there was no sign of them. After a short break, they continued up the mountain to the village of Drenovë. Johnny convinced the villagers to give the Americans a place to stay for the night. Of course aiding them was a great danger to the villagers. After witnessing the brutal Nazi attack, the Americans understood that danger. They were very grateful for the help the villagers offered.

That night the group sat by a fire and ate cornbread provided by the owner of the house. In the dim light, they wondered aloud what had happened to the rest of their group. Perhaps they had been in the trucks when they were strafed by the planes. Perhaps they'd been captured. Indeed, all of them seemed to be in grave danger of being captured at any moment.

WHAT SHOULD THEY DO NOW?

Thrasher and Baggs thought they should stay in the village and wait to see if the rest of the group caught up with them. They began to burn their identification and all information that might hint at who they were – just in case they were caught. Jensen had written Steffa's name and address down so that she could reach him after the war, but now she tossed it into the fire. If she was caught with his information, he would be killed.

Hayes, Owen and some other medics argued that they should keep hiking up the mountain, towards the sea. Staying put could mean being caught. If they ran, at least they had a chance. The medics went outside for a private meeting. When they returned they told the group that they planned to leave in the morning whether the others joined them or not. Thrasher thought about it for a few moments, and then he agreed with their plan.

· · · · ·

Orville Abbott was with Steffa and a group of other Americans when the tank came towards them on the road out of Berat. They hid in the tall brush and waited. While they waited, all of them held their breath in fear – all of them except one of the nurses, Pauleen Kanable, from Wisconsin, USA. Abbott watched, impressed, as Kanable pulled out a little mirror and fixed her make-up. Perhaps she was only distracting herself from her nervousness, but one thing was certain. This was one tough American woman he was trapped with.

After a time, the vehicles rolled away, and Steffa stood up. It was time for them to hike away from town, and quickly. The Americans were reluctant, not knowing where the rest of their group was, but Steffa insisted they move. The others were being led by one of his men, and Steffa promised they would all meet up again soon. Though the Americans protested more, eventually they gave in. What other choice did they have?

Besides Steffa, Abbott and Kanable, the group included nurses Gertrude "Tooie" Dawson, Ann Markowitz, Jean Rutkowski and medics John Wolf, Paul Allen, Gilbert Hornsby and Robert Cranson. The limping Shumway was with them too. They slowly made their way up the mountain. After hiking for about three hours, they came across a settlement where some Italian soldiers were living. After Steffa talked with the Italian colonel, food was brought for the Americans – bread and anchovies, with a single egg for each of them. Abbott put his egg in his pocket, hoping it wouldn't break and that he could cook it later.

They ate and rested for 20 minutes before heading
up the mountain again. Some Italian soldiers went with
them for protection. As they walked, they asked Steffa
about the Nazi raid. Though Steffa did not think the
Nazis had known that the Americans were in the town,
he agreed that they probably did now. All the propaganda
photos hung about the town would ensure that. They
hadn't seen any sign of the other group of Americans,
nor had the Italians. But Steffa told the Americans he was
certain they were following close behind.

· · · · ·

Neither group of Americans knew it, but three
of the nurses had not made it out of Berat. Ann
Maness, Helen Porter and Wilma Lytle were staying
in a farmhouse on the edge of town. Their hosts

were a farmer called Nani Karaja, his wife, Goni, their school-age nephew, Koli and Nani's mother, who was called "Mama Ollga".

When the Nazis started shelling that morning, Nani told the women to stay hidden in the farmhouse, which they did. They peeked out from a quilt that was hung over the window and watched as some of the soldiers made camp on the grounds of a school across the street from them. The women didn't dare move.

It turned out that the soldiers were not Germans but Hungarians who had been recruited into the Nazi army. It also turned out that they knew the nurses were in the farmhouse. Later that day, two of the Hungarian soldiers came over to investigate. They asked a few questions. Though they didn't speak Hungarian, the Americans were able to communicate that they were nurses. The soldiers told them to stay put in the farmhouse.

The women had no idea if the soldiers had been paid off somehow, perhaps by partisans, so they would not be captured. Or perhaps the Hungarians were taking the opportunity to resist their German leaders. Maybe they were simply being kind. Whatever the case, the three nurses did as they were told and stayed in the farmhouse.

CHAPTER 6

KEEP CLIMBING

Steffa, Abbott and the rest of their group hiked deeper into the mountains with the Italian soldiers for protection. At nightfall, they arrived in a small village, and Steffa spoke to the village elder. He indicated that the Americans were an invasion force sent to liberate the Albanians. The Americans were uncomfortable with this lie continuing to be spread about them, but using the story, Steffa secured a place to sleep and some cornbread and cheese to eat.

While they ate, Steffa told them that the male lead in the musical they'd seen the previous night had been shot back in Berat by the Germans. He'd been trying to defend the village.

"Last night he sings; he is beautiful," Steffa said.

Clearly this was sad news, and it added to the discomfort of the Americans. They began to wonder about Steffa. If he knew that the singer had been killed in Berat, why didn't he know anything about the rest of the Americans? Maybe he knew more than he was telling them. Maybe he wasn't on their side at all. Maybe he was leading them into a trap. What did they know about Steffa anyway? Why should they trust him?

They pressed Steffa again about the other Americans. This time, Steffa said they would catch up in about an hour.

If this was reassuring to Abbott and the others, they didn't feel comforted for long. In the morning, after a night of very little sleep, the others had not caught up to them. Now Steffa told them their friends were several hours behind.

The Americans decided they needed to confront Steffa. Because the nurses were officers and held rank over the enlisted men, two of them approached him. Tooie Dawson and Ann Markowitz told Steffa they needed some answers. They told him that if the others were only hours behind, they wanted to wait to move on until they reunited. According to Steffa, the others weren't coming this way.

Seeing little alternative, they followed Steffa's advice and continued to hike higher into the mountains, putting distance between themselves and the Germans.

Their suspicions about Steffa grew after dinner the next night when he told them the rest of the Americans were coming soon. Members of the Liberation Army had seen them this morning.

Dawson, Abbott and the other Americans weren't sure whether to believe this news. After all, Steffa had been evasive and, when it came to the other group of Americans, wrong. It was not surprising when, as the night wore on, the other group did not show up.

Abbott's frustration boiled over. "Okay, Steffa," he said, "what's the story now? It's past 10 o' clock and they aren't here. We want to know why and we want to know right now."

Steffa told them he didn't know. That got Tooie Dawson riled up. "I believe you," she exclaimed. "And I doubt if you even know where they are."

Sensing that the Americans were frustrated with him, he reminded them that they were all friends.

"We're not your friends! We are your prisoners!" Dawson exclaimed.

Whatever they were, the Americans still didn't see any option other than to keep climbing to freedom.

• • • • •

The group that was travelling with Johnny woke up early the next morning after the attack on Berat. Two Albanians entered the room where they were sleeping in the village of Drenovë and motioned for them to leave – now. Johnny leapt to his feet and joined in leading the Americans out of the house while the two Albanians paced nervously. With all the German activity in the area, it was very dangerous for them to be found helping Americans. The sooner they left, the sooner the locals would be safe.

The group quickly gathered the little gear they had and scrambled up the trail. After they'd made some distance from the village, Baggs and Jensen stopped Johnny to have a talk. They wanted to know where the rest of the Americans were.

"Does this trail lead to a village where we're likely to find them?" Jensen asked Johnny.

But Johnny didn't seem to understand, so Baggs went over the story again of how they'd been separated from a group of other Americans.

"Ah, ten more!" Johnny said then. "Yes, come with me."

CHAPTER 7

REUNITED

Jensen, Baggs and the others followed Johnny
up the trail, hoping that he knew something about
their friends. Soon they ran into a large band of men
dressed in run-down Italian army uniforms. After the
Americans passed the men, the rag-tag soldiers began
to follow them at a distance up the trail. Jensen thought
they made a comical "little army".

They hiked for several hours, growing tired, thirsty
and hungry. Once, when they were taking a break,
an Italian officer approached Jensen and, in decent

English, introduced himself. He said he was a major in the medical corps and recognized the medical insignia on the Americans' uniforms. What were they doing in Albania?

Jensen told him the story of their crash and their journey so far, and then she asked if he'd seen the rest of the Americans. He had not. When Jensen asked what he and his men were doing in Albania, he told her that they'd been stranded here after Italy surrendered in September. Their own nation had sent nobody to help them get home. They believed they would have better luck joining the Americans, who surely would be rescued by someone. They didn't know how dicey the Americans' luck had been so far.

Rain began to fall as they continued on their hike, climbing a steep embankment. It was hardly a trail at all – rather, they were climbing up slabs of slate that were slick with the rain. They climbed and at times crawled as necessary. Jensen's fingers and knees were sliced and gashed as she went.

Suddenly gunfire rang out from several different directions. A bullet buzzed terrifyingly close to Jensen's head. She dropped to the ground and began to crawl away from the shots as fast as she could. Baggs pointed to a stone house up the hill, and they all crawled towards it. A few tried to stand up and run, but bullets spattered the dirt around them, so they dropped again into a crawl.

When they reached the house, they took shelter against a stone wall. They worked out that some of the shots were coming from the town behind them while others were coming from a village across a ravine. The group was caught in a crossfire.

One at a time, they crawled to the door of the house and slid inside. "Stay close to the floor," Baggs said. Crouching down, they asked Johnny if it was Germans shooting.

"Maybe Ballista!" he said. Ballista, or Ballists, were Albanians who were not part of the resistance. They fought for the Germans. This was the first that Jensen had heard of this group.

"Oh, great," she said sarcastically. If fleeing from Nazis wasn't hard enough, they also had to worry about the Ballista. More bad luck!

They laid low for a while, but they didn't want to be in the house when night came. The fighters could approach the building under cover of dark and toss a grenade through the window.

Before they could make a plan of escape, though, two Albanians burst through the door with a third man who was bleeding badly from a gunshot wound in his leg. His trouser leg was soaked with blood and he'd bitten through his lip trying to distract himself from the pain in his leg. Jensen gave him morphine for the pain, then she cleaned and dressed the wound, though she didn't think he'd live through the day.

The shooting continued outside irregularly. Johnny sneaked down to where the partisans were hiding just below them on the mountain. He was gone for a few minutes, and when he came back, he had a plan. The partisans would wait until one hour before sundown and then barrage the Ballista with a shower of gunfire that would allow the Americans to escape. They gathered their supplies and got ready. At the appointed time, the shots erupted as promised, and the group hurried from the building past the shooters and the jangle of gunfire. Having no way to help or transport the injured man, they were forced to leave him in the stone house.

The distraction worked, and they escaped to the cover of a low stone wall. Jensen hoped that Johnny knew where they were going as they made their way up the mountain, hiking through the rain for several hours. The Americans were shivering in damp clothes and feeling their way along the trail in darkness. When the rain finally let up, the Americans turned to see how far they'd come. Below them, they saw the glittering lights of Berat, not nearly as far away as they felt the city should be after the journey they'd had.

They hiked in the dark without hearing any shooting or other noises except for a few barking dogs. Around midnight, they took shelter in an empty stone barn near a village called Kapitonë. Wet, cold and exhausted, the women and men lay down to sleep in the hay. But they slept for only a few hours before Johnny woke them. It was time to move on. The Italians who'd been following them were out of sight, and he wanted to get away from them while they had the chance. Hiking with such a large group of uniformed soldiers was a good way to get more Ballista shooting at you.

Jensen was moving a little slower that morning because of dysentery. She, like everyone else, was distracted by hunger, thirst and heaving stomach pain.

All day the group travelled up the mountain, stopping in every village along the way to ask if anyone had seen the other Americans. Nobody had. Near nightfall, Johnny asked at one of the villages for a place to stay for the night. At first they were turned away. Johnny kept talking, though, and soon the Americans were inside a small house with a fire.

They were fed a baked onion dish. It may not have been five-star food, but it was the first food they'd had in two days. The group slept under blankets in the tight, warm room. It was more luxury than they'd had since leaving Berat.

The next day they continued on their journey, though Jensen was still not sure where they were going. The difficulty of communicating with Johnny, the constant begging for food and their exhaustion made everyone feel helpless and frustrated. In addition, the dysentery from which many of them suffered was causing severe diarrhoea. Still, they walked all day, arriving in another village after dark. Johnny arranged a hot meal of white bean stew and a place for everyone to sleep. Jensen thought beans had never tasted so good. She slept deeply but not long. They were back on the trail at dawn.

After hiking for two hours that morning, they finally got some encouraging news. They arrived in a village where Johnny again asked about the other group of Americans. This time, the answer was different. The old man replied that he'd heard about some Americans staying in a village called Dobrushë, which was about three hours away. He also had some darker news. The villagers believed the man they were travelling with, Steffa, was working for the Germans. He was not to be trusted, the man said.

This seemed at odds with what Jensen knew about Steffa. Why would he have taken them under his wing if he didn't want to help them? He'd had chances to turn them all in before, but he had not done it. All Jensen could do was hope that the old villager was wrong about Steffa.

Thrilled that their friends were so near, they set out with renewed energy towards their new destination. They weren't sure if the old man was correct about the other Americans. And even if he was right, the others may have moved on – maybe they weren't in Dobrushë any longer. They tried to keep their hopes in check as they climbed a steep switchback trail. The mountains around them were jagged and towering, reminding them of the peaks they'd flown over a week ago, before their crash. The group stopped often to catch their breath.

After a few hours, they reached the top of a ridge. In the distance, a village was visible – Dobrushë. They picked their way down the trail, and soon they saw American uniforms in the distance. They'd found the others! Running now, they closed the distance to the village.

In front of the hospital where they'd been staying, Ann Markowitz and Jean Rutkowski began yelling,

"They're here! They're here!" Dawson, Abbott, Steffa and the others poured out of the hospital, and soon the group was reunited. Everyone was hugging and shaking hands in celebration, walking back into the hospital. Suddenly, the happiness was broken when one of the women said, "Where's Porter?"

"My God, isn't she with you?" Thrasher asked.

"And where's Lytle and Maness?" someone else asked.

They counted heads and realized that the group was not totally reunited. Nobody had seen Lytle, Maness or Porter since the night before the attack in Berat.

As Steffa shook hands with Jensen and the other members of her group, the nurse must have felt a darkening mood pass over everyone while they each chatted and told one another where they'd been. The nurses in Steffa's group told Jensen about their argument with him the night before. Steffa had wanted to move on, but the Americans had fought to stay and wait. Tooie Dawson had been particularly feisty, and eventually Steffa agreed to stay. They were glad he did. For now, Jensen decided not to tell her friends what the villager had said about Steffa. They had more important things to worry about – like how to find the three missing nurses.

Their first idea was to head back to Berat to find them, but that was quickly shot down. It would be too dangerous with the Germans in control of the town. Steffa said that he would try to find out information about the three nurses. However, with the Nazis in control of the area, it would be nearly impossible to rescue them. He said he'd heard the village was running out of food. Besides, the Americans' photos were posted all over Berat. The Germans were sure to recognize any of them who dared to go back. Finally,

Steffa said he would send someone back to Berat to scout for answers and catch up to the group later. Everyone agreed this was the best course of action.

Jensen's spirits perked up when she learned that there was a fresh stream nearby. Rutkowski showed her and the other nurses that had been in Johnny's group the way, recommending that they all bathe and fill their canteens. The fresh water must have felt amazing after so many days of being sick and cut up, sleeping on dirty floors, cleaning bloody wounds, and crawling up a mountainside.

While the nurses cleaned up at the stream, the newly reconciled women compared their stories. Markowitz described how Steffa told them to get back on the truck after everyone abandoned it the first time. Jensen and her group had stayed hidden.

"Steffa told you to get back on the truck?" asked Jensen.

"Yeah," Markowitz replied.

When the German planes came in, Markowitz and the group with her barely got off the truck in time before it was riddled with bullets.

Jensen listened to the story with growing apprehension. She shared what the man at the village had said about Steffa. Should they continue to trust him? Rutkowski and Markowitz admitted that they'd had concerns about Steffa too.

In spite of their suspicions, everyone felt better when Steffa said that they could buy a goat to roast. Would the Americans be interested? They certainly would! Baggs paid for the goat with their pooled money, and it was slaughtered and cooked. But once again the Americans were to be disappointed. The goat had hardly enough meat on its bones to make a stew.

Their meal consisted mostly of cornbread – again.

Everyone craved heartier food.

After they ate, Steffa mentioned the British

officers again. They were not far away, he said. The

Americans were tired, thirsty and worried about the

missing women. Many of them also were still sick

with diarrhoea, and they were grumpy about the goat.

But Steffa's words about the British was the best news

they'd heard in a long time. Jensen only hoped his

words were true.

CHAPTER 8

BLIZZARD!

That night they slept in Dobrushë. Unfortunately, the blankets the locals gave them were infested with fleas and lice, adding to the growing list of illnesses and hardships the Americans faced. Harold Hayes still had some louse powder, and he used it to combat them. But many of the others had left their medical bags behind when the Germans attacked Berat. They suffered from intense itching.

Adding to their discomfort, they kept thinking about the missing nurses. Were they okay? Had they been captured? Were they even alive? Everyone felt intense guilt for having left them behind.

In the morning, after yet another night of insufficient sleep, some of the nurses returned to the stream to clean up and brush their teeth. When they got back, Johnny was saying goodbye. He would be heading in a different direction. Jensen and the others from their group thanked him for his help. Despite all the mistrust and difficulty communicating, they would miss him.

The Americans pressed Steffa about the British officers. He admitted that he didn't know exactly where they were, only that there was probably an officer in one of three villages up the mountain. He also didn't know who it was. "Maybe a general," he said when they asked.

They agreed to send a messenger ahead with a note for the officer. Jensen gave up one of the small slips of paper she had been writing on to record the details of their journey. Thrasher wrote and signed the note that contained vague information in case it was intercepted by Germans. It would let the British know what was going on, especially if they had heard about the crash. But the Germans wouldn't gain any valuable information about them. Thrasher signed it with only his initials. Steffa gave the note to one of the guides, and he ran ahead to find the officers.

Abbott was among those who still doubted Steffa's intentions. Since Steffa gave his instructions to the messenger in Albanian, Abbot wasn't even sure the messenger would try to deliver the note. But, Abbott concluded, it was the best chance they had. Maybe they'd get lucky.

Abbott was already feeling sad when Paul Allen, a hunter like Abbott, began talking about life in his home state of Kentucky, USA. If they were in Kentucky, he said, they'd have plenty of wild game to shoot.

"We'd be living off the fat of the land and not worrying if we ever got out," he said.

That was too much for Abbott. "Shut up! Before I burst out crying!" he said.

• • • • •

The villagers in Dobrushë were eager for the Americans to clear out. The area was crawling with Germans and Ballista. Steffa led the group towards a small village about a thousand metres up the mountain. He reasoned that nobody would be likely to chase them up such treacherous territory. That was the good news. The bad news was that it was such treacherous territory.

Steffa and the Americans trudged up the mountainside trail, stopping often to rest and catch their breath. Many of them began to suffer from altitude sickness. Oxygen was thin.

The area where they climbed was known as the Albanian Alps, with each mountain peak more jagged and threatening than the last. Each time they made the top of one summit, they were deflated to realize they only had to climb another.

During a rest, they assessed their situation. They had fleas, lice, diarrhoea, and countless cuts and bruises. Due to the altitude sickness, many of them were throwing up just off the side of the trail. Many, including Jensen, were scurrying often into the bushes for their diarrhoea. They were all hungry and thirsty. They were cold, and the higher they got, the colder it got. Their shoes were wearing out – especially those of the women, which were not made for this kind of travel. But if any of the medics feared that the women wouldn't be able to keep up, those fears were put to rest. The women were as tough and determined as the men.

One piece of good news was that Shumway, the airman who'd been injured in the crash landing, was walking on his own now, albeit with a limp.

That afternoon, when the sun sank behind the mountains, the group was immediately blanketed in darkness. They followed Steffa, groping along the narrow shelf of a trail, aware that a false step could result in a long, dangerous tumble. Jensen thought they looked like a line of baby ducks following their mother.

At last they arrived at a village called Derzhezha, coughing and gasping to catch their breath. Dogs barked and people stepped out of their homes to see who was coming.

"Steffa was sure right about this place," Paul Allen said. The Germans wouldn't be chasing them up here. "I doubt any of them would want to make this climb."

Two village elders came up and spoke with Steffa. They had a long, intense conversation, and the Americans began to worry that they wouldn't be allowed to stay. Finally, though, Steffa told them that they'd have a place to sleep tonight – but only tonight. The villagers fed them a small meal, and in the morning they were off again.

Again, they hiked up and down steep, difficult trails, gaining a little altitude as they went. In the early afternoon, they stopped at a village called Leshnija. As usual, Steffa spoke with the village elders. When they were finished, Steffa told the airmen what he'd learned. Earlier that day, scouts from the village had learned that Ballists and Germans were in the area and heading towards them. The Americans were invited to stay for one night, but then they needed to leave quickly.

That night they were fed a dinner of onions and bread. Many had trouble holding it down due to their stomach problems. As they settled in to sleep, Jensen worried about the medics, who had only light jackets for warmth. She gave her coat liner to Charles Zeiber to wear overnight. "Just don't forget to pick up my liner as you leave if we get routed in a hurry during the night," she said. She had overheard what Steffa said about the enemy being in the area.

Jensen set her shoes and socks next to the fire to dry. Though the group had suffered much, they were growing close. Probably their budding friendship and loyalty to one another helped keep them going. As Jensen drifted off to sleep, her teeth chattered from the cold or perhaps, she thought, from a fever.

• • • • •

The group began hiking the next day, accompanied
by guides Steffa had hired to help them climb the
high peak of Mount Tomorrit. It was their 14th day in
Albania, in late November, and the days were short and
cold. Things were about to get even more harsh.

As they set out up the mountain, the trail was
covered with a dusting of snow. But as the day went on,
freezing rain began to fall, turning the rugged path into
a muddy mess. While the Americans took a break, two
Albanians caught up to them and talked with Thrasher.
Abbott and the others watched, and then Thrasher
turned to the group. Abbott felt everyone tense up. This
was not going to be good.

"These two men have come after a certain stone,"
Thrasher said. Somebody had stolen it from the village

they'd stayed in a couple of nights earlier. "They say this stone is very old and very powerful," Thrasher explained. It was supposed to bring medicine to the villagers, but bad luck to anyone who took it.

At first, nobody said anything. At last, Bill Eldridge, a medic from Kentucky, pulled the stone in question from his pocket. "I guess this is it," he admitted. He had wanted to keep it as a souvenir.

Thrasher took the stone and thanked Bill sarcastically. The Albanians had told him that whoever took it would die. "But maybe it'll lift the bad luck off the rest of us," he said.

Abbott recalls that the tension faded then, almost as quickly as it had come, and the group set off on the trail again, perhaps thinking about their luck. By afternoon, snow swirled in the air, and then a black storm cloud moved over them. Suddenly, a stiff wind rose up with sheets of blinding snow. The hikers couldn't see one another, nor could they see much off the side of the trail. But they knew it was a steep drop. One false step, and they'd fall a long way.

Yelling over the ferocious wind, Jensen asked Jim Cruise to rush to the front of the line and ask Steffa and the guides to slow down. It was too hard to keep up under these conditions, and she was afraid she was falling too far behind. She took off her gloves and rubbed her hands together and saw Rutkowski lying on the ground. Two of the men went to help her up, but she seemed to have given up. She asked the others to leave her there to die.

"We're all going through!" Baggs yelled. "Come on, you'll make it once you're up. You must keep moving, Jean. We all must keep moving!"

"No," Rutkowski replied. "I can't take another step."

"Get up!" Baggs yelled back.

He and Paul Allen lifted her and helped her along. Just as she got moving, Tooie Dawson slipped and fell and began to slide down the mountain. Gilbert Hornsby lunged after her and stopped her from sliding farther. Digging his boots into the snow, he began to pull her back to the trail. Jensen helped him, and eventually everyone was on the trail again. They were covered in snow and utterly exhausted.

At that point, the line came to a stop. Cruise and Abbott reached the front of the line, where Steffa was yelling at one of the guides. Apparently the guide was refusing to go on. He wanted to wait for the storm to end. But Steffa was having none of it. Abbott wrote later of how Steffa got in the guide's face and talked to him in a very serious, low tone. Abbott didn't understand the language, but he got the feeling that Steffa was threatening the guide's life if he didn't continue leading – and now. Steffa shoved him ahead, and they kept going, one weary step at a time.

"I think that at the time most of us expected death was within the hour for the whole party," Abbott recalled. At the same time, their feelings towards Steffa may have shifted as well. He had probably saved their lives by forcing the guide to continue.

They trudged forward. Jensen wiggled her fingers and toes to keep the blood flowing through them. Then, just as suddenly as the storm had begun, it stopped. The wind cut off, and the driving snow turned again into pleasant swirls. Jensen looked back at the black cloud under which they'd passed. A ray of sun broke through the storm.

The trail began to slope downhill, and they followed it to the village of Terlioria. It was only about 3 p.m., meaning they'd been on the trail for about six hours.

They'd been in the blizzard for less than one hour. It all

seemed much longer to the miserable Americans.

As they came into the village, the locals came out and

greeted them with amazement. They couldn't believe

they'd climbed Mount Tomorrit in a blizzard. The

Americans were quickly divided up into homes where

they took off their wet clothes and hung them by fires

to dry. Jensen, Elna Schwant and Jean Rutkowski were

given a wooden tub of warm water in which to warm

their feet. Everyone had a warm meal of mutton stew

accompanied by the usual cornbread.

About 24 hours after they'd arrived in Terlioria, the

runner who'd gone ahead to find the British returned.

Thrasher took the note he brought back and got a huge

grin on his face. He ran to all the different houses and

read the note to everyone.

Sorry to hear of your misfortune. The hospital at Catania has been informed of your whereabouts – wheels are in progress for your swift evacuation to civilization.

... Since you're heading this way, you may as well come to Lavdar, where I shall plan to meet you on 01 December, or as soon as I receive word that you are there. We can make plans for your evacuation then.

The letter was signed by someone called Smith of the British Forces.

Everyone was thrilled. They danced and hugged and patted each other on the back. They repeated words to each other, "Evacuation!" "Wheels are in motion!"

"How far is Lavdar?" Schwant asked.

"Not far," Steffa said. It would take them a couple of days to get there.

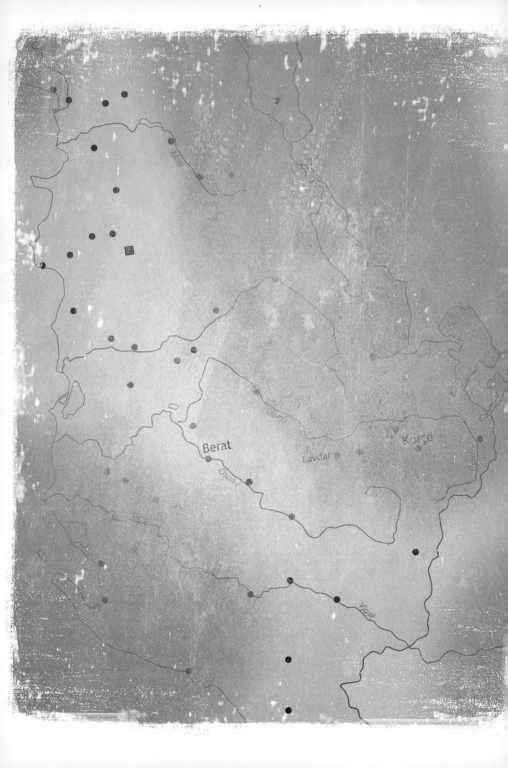

CHAPTER 9

HELP FROM THE BRITISH

The Americans stayed in Terlioria for two more days, until the bad weather died down. When they left it was Thursday, 25 November. In the United States, it was Thanksgiving.

They walked for about three days over terrain that was flatter than that which they'd been taking until now. It must have seemed almost leisurely compared to the harrowing trails they'd come up before. The sole of Jensen's shoe was coming off, and she had to step high to avoid bending it back.

Joining them for this stretch of the trip was a partisan leader called Pandee who spoke some English and apparently held a high rank among the partisans. They slept the first night in a little hamlet. Eager to get back on the trail the next morning, they were getting ready to go when they heard a rumbling sound in the sky. Nazi planes flew towards them quite low, and everyone dived for cover, hoping they hadn't been seen. It was a solemn reminder that so little was in their control. As long as they were in Albania, their luck could shift at any second.

Once they were sure the planes weren't coming back, they gathered again on the trail and left for Lavdar. They arrived in Lavdar around midday. There, standing and smiling in the road, was a man in a clean, crisp British uniform. The Americans rushed to shake his hand as he continued beaming.

"I'm Captain Smith," he said.

The Americans could hardly believe it. There really was a British officer in Albania who could help them. Captain Victor Smith led them into a one-room building with a roaring fire and made a list of everyone's name, rank and serial number. The Americans told him everything they'd been through so far. They also told him about the missing nurses, whom they presumed were still hiding in Berat. Smith said he would report all this to his superiors, who would relay the information to American officials.

• • • • •

Captain Victor Smith was an officer in the British clandestine action agency, the SOE. The SOE had been working with the partisans in Albania to fight the Nazis who were occupying the country.

Before the war broke out, Albania had fallen under Italian rule, and many Albanians were already engaging in guerilla tactics to resist the Italians. When Italy surrendered to the Allies in 1943, the Germans moved in hoping to shore up the territory. But the partisans, who had been united into a single army under General Hoxha, continued to resist and gave the Germans much more trouble than expected. This was good news for the Allies, as the Germans had to devote more troops to the area. That meant they had fewer troops to fight elsewhere around the globe. And that's why the SOE was helping the partisans. By doing so, they were weakening Nazi forces elsewhere and increasing the chance that the Allies would win the war.

The partisans were doing a pretty good job of frustrating the Germans. They had weapons provided by the British and training from officers such as Smith. The partisans were killing Nazis and Ballists, blowing up bridges and roads important to Nazi movements and destroying or stealing vehicles. They attacked enemy convoys, intercepted supplies, and disrupted the Nazis' communications with neighbouring Greece. In villages all over the country, men and women alike fought fiercely for the right to keep their country out of fascist control. Along with the actual fighting, there was also an ongoing fight for hearts and minds.

As Jensen, Baggs and the other Americans who'd been travelling with Johnny discovered outside of Drenovë, not all Albanians were partisans. Some sided with the Nazis and fought to help them tighten down control of the nation. Still other Albanians were not loyal to either group.

The Americans wouldn't learn about this until after they were safely home, but General Hoxha had told Hasan Gina and Kostig Steffa to bring them to as many villages as possible to show them off. The Americans were propaganda meant to prove how strong Hoxha's alliance with the Allies was. Look! he was saying. They have sent an invasion force to support us in our fight to be free from the fascists. The hope was that the locals would see this show of strength and join up with the partisans.

When the Americans described to Captain Smith the journey they'd taken so far, Smith questioned Steffa. "Why did you bring these people all the way here?" he asked. Lavdar was east of where they'd landed and close to Greece, which was heavily occupied by the Germans. It would have been much wiser to bring them west towards the coast, where they could escape by boat to Italy.

Steffa explained that much of the territory was occupied by Ballista, and he was doing his best to keep them safe first.

Smith reminded Steffa that there were other officers near Berat. If they'd contacted the British there, they could have been evacuated much more easily – perhaps they'd be back in Italy by now. Hearing this, the Americans were stunned and frustrated.

Their feelings became more positive, though, when Smith told them that the SOE had begun devising an escape plan. The plan was simple if not easy. They would hike across the country to the coast of the Adriatic Sea, where a boat would take them to Bari. It would take a long time to make it across the country, with the first stop on the trip being an SOE base in a nearby town called Krushovë, where they would load up with supplies that were being dropped in by parachute. But first they would stay here in Lavdar to rest and regain their strength for a couple of days.

• • • • •

Back in Berat, Ann Maness, Helen Porter and Wilma Lytle were safe. They remained, hiding and waiting, in the same farmhouse where they had stayed their first night there. They had not seen the other Americans in two weeks.

Nani and his brother, Kiçi, were wine makers and had done business with some of the Germans. As such, they were able to convince the Germans to ignore the nurses in their home. The women passed the time by playing cards and helping with the household chores. They ate well and were kept safe, but they were bored.

· · · · ·

Back in Lavdar, it was time to move out. But many in the party were sicker than ever with dysentery. To make things easier, Captain Smith rented six mules and ordered Bob Owen and Paul Allen to ride two of them – the two medics were severely nauseous. Two other mules were loaded with supplies. Later on the journey, which required them to hike through knee-high snow, Bill Eldridge, Lillian Tacina and Ann Kopsco were placed on mules as well due to freezing feet.

Upon arriving in Krushovë, they were dispersed into different homes, as usual, to eat and sleep. Captain Smith visited everyone and handed out supplies that had arrived, starting with several pairs of heavy wool socks as well as fresh army boots. Everyone quickly realized that they were unlikely to find perfect fits, with all the socks being huge and the boots being in a random range of sizes, but even so they were thrilled with the warm new footwear. A local cobbler fixed many of the Americans' shoes in case they couldn't find boots that fit. They retreaded the worn-out shoes by affixing old tyre treads to the soles.

Most nights, British planes flew noisily overhead and dropped supplies in by parachute. But although their supplies were improving, most of the Americans continued to suffer from diarrhoea and vomiting. They had lice and fleas. Smith decided to keep everyone in Krushovë for a few more days until they all felt better. Abbott and some of the other medics played lots of poker with an old, sticky deck of cards that someone had lugged all over the countryside in his bag. And they dreamed about what their escape would look like when it finally happened – and what they'd do when they got home.

On Friday, 3 December, Jensen realized it was her birthday, and she let the others know. She was 29. Smith and some others found butter, cream and sugar in the village and made homemade ice cream, freezing it in a snow bank, and surprised her with it.

• • • • •

Over the days, a few more British officers parachuted in, and others came in over land. One of the newcomers was Lieutenant Gavan Duffy, a tall, stiff man with dark hair and eyes and a distinct moustache. Duffy was a demolition expert who was teaching partisans how to blow up bridges, roads and Nazi vehicles. His father died when Duffy was a boy, so Duffy had worked in construction from a young age to help his family get by. He developed a strong

mechanical aptitude, and when he joined up with the
Royal Engineers, he also developed a knack for making
bombs and laying mines.

Duffy had heard about the stranded Americans
shortly after they crash-landed, and he'd been trying
to catch up with them ever since. As they chatted with
Duffy, the Americans began to gain an appreciation for
the massive effort the Brits were putting into Albania in
general and into rescuing them especially. Duffy was a
whizz with weapons, explosives and mechanics – and he
survived in the wilds of Albania on his own.

Duffy did have some help from an intelligence officer
called Jon Naar, who was stationed in Cairo. Naar's
expertise was intelligence. He spoke German, French
and passable Russian and Arabic. Naar coordinated the
British movements on a map covered with drawing pins.
He tracked Nazi and Ballista movements and helped

coordinate attacks on the Nazis.

Duffy explained that with Naar's help, he and his assistant, Sergeant Herbert Bell, would lead the Americans to safety. Joining them would be Steffa, Pandee and several armed guerillas. An American officer, Captain Lloyd Smith, had left Bari and was heading their way. He'd meet them in the mountains and take them the rest of the way to a coastal hideout called Seaview.

The Americans were delighted to finally have a straightforward plan after three weeks of what seemed like blind wandering.

CHAPTER 10

DUFFY AND HIS CHICKENS

Orville Abbott had been troubled by the thought of his mum at home in Michigan receiving the news that he was missing. For weeks now, she had heard nothing more. She must have been wracked with worry. Indeed, all of the Americans were concerned about how their families were handling the news. It must be hard to know that your child is out in the world somewhere, most likely in grave danger – possibly dead.

But Smith was able to bring some relief to Abbott and the rest. Now that the Americans had been found, he sent word that they were safe – all but

three of them – to the Allies. Telegrams were then sent

to family members letting them know the news. The

telegrams contained no detail, only that the Americans

were "safe now and accounted for". That would be

welcome news for the families.

• • • • •

On the evening of Tuesday, 7 December, the

American Office of Strategic Services (OSS) officer,

Captain Lloyd Smith, set out by boat from Brindisi, Italy,

towards the coast of Albania. He rode as a passenger in

a fishing boat and was dressed in an airman's uniform.

In case he was discovered by Germans, he hoped they

would believe he was a downed pilot. The Nazis were

likely to kill him if they thought he was a spy, but a pilot might become a prisoner of war.

Smith's superiors had prepared him for this mission with only a three-hour informational session. His grasp of the complicated fighting between Ballista and the factions that made up the Albanian National Liberation Army was hazy, much like his understanding of the land. Adding to his disadvantage was the fact that he spoke no Albanian at all. He'd be relying heavily on translators and guides and highly detailed maps provided by the SOE.

Smith had attempted before to get across, but the waterway was crawling with Germans. Another attempt was thwarted by bad weather. Tonight, though, Smith's boat anchored about 800 metres offshore, and a crew rowed him to shore along with a cache of supplies. Smith hiked up a trail to Seaview, a collection of caves in the cliffs where the SOE had set up a base a few weeks earlier. It was equipped with bunk beds and a

stove. A radio put them in touch with the SOE in Bari,

Cairo and elsewhere. The cave was also stocked with

weapons and ammunition.

Several SOE members lived in the caves, as did a

couple of Americans and an Albanian guide. This group

formed a crucial link in an intelligence network that

kept Allied forces appraised of actions in Albania. Smith

unloaded his supplies in the camp and waited to hear

about the Americans' progress.

$$\bullet \ \bullet \ \bullet \ \bullet \ \bullet$$

On Wednesday morning, the day after the American

Smith landed at Seaview, the group of stranded nurses

and medics left Krushovë, heading towards the sea

at last. The Americans were impressed with Duffy,

who was strong, fit and confident, and who seemed
unaffected by the long hikes. Before leaving, he warned
them to obey his orders without question – Germans
and Ballista were everywhere, and they'd have to
be careful. With that, he and Bell led the way. Bell's
wireless radio was strapped onto the back of one of the
mules Duffy had bought for the trip.

As they hiked single-file through the snow, Duffy
occasionally looked back to check on his followers. His
hand was always on the handle of his MP40 machine
gun. Sometimes Duffy stood aside and let them pass
as if inspecting them. "Counting his chickens," Jensen
called it.

Soon the group stopped for a break in a small,
burned-out village that had been destroyed by fighting
a few weeks earlier. In spite of the damage, villagers
were still living in the wrecked homes, and Duffy was

able to buy some bread and goats' cheese. While they ate, Bell radioed ahead to arrange for a place to stay that night in the village of Gjergjevicë. Their night in that village was not pleasant. There was little food to share, and, again, the blankets were infested with lice.

As the men lay in bed in a home, Owen told the group that it was his 21st birthday. Thousands of kilometres away from home, the young man must have been longing even more than usual to see his family that night.

Bill Eldridge continued to battle nausea, and he didn't sleep much. Yet in the morning, Duffy informed the group that they would be hiking at an even brisker pace that day. Eldridge was ordered onto a mule. They reached a small village called Panarit that night, where Jensen and a few of the other nurses took care of Eldridge. They gave him a shot of morphine and extra coats to sleep under.

Lebo and Shumway stayed in a home that was hosting a wedding party. They were up late partying with locals. The next morning, Lebo and Shumway told funny stories about the singing, dancing and even fighting that had occurred at the home in which they stayed. It must have been strange to hear about the celebration – a normal, happy part of life – while the castaways feared for their own lives. In any event, Abbott later wrote that the wedding stories entertained the group for several long kilometres of their hike, helping to distract them from their troubles.

· · · · ·

On the third day, Duffy was forced to change his route as they approached an area heavily occupied by Ballista. At one village, they stopped to talk to the partisans living there. The partisans explained that less than an hour away was a Ballista village. Everyone was on edge. As Duffy led them along the trail, they passed by armed partisans preparing to fight. Worried about getting caught in a firefight, Duffy and the Americans rushed through the area as quickly as they could.

Their new route led them up a very steep mountain to a dangerous river crossing. Weeks earlier, partisans had blown up the only reliable crossing. Now the only way across was on a rickety suspension bridge swinging from ropes. With snipers and machine gunners possibly hiding in the area, Duffy hid the group near the end of the bridge and sent them across in small groups. Four or five at a time, the Americans were told to hustle down the path and rush quickly across the rattling bridge.

Everyone made it without being shot at. Even the gear, which had to be unloaded from the mules and carried across on foot, made it. On the far side, they were loaded onto a creaky old Italian truck, which drove them a few kilometres to Përmet, another village that had been attacked and burned down by Germans.

But in spite of the town's impoverished conditions, the Americans were greeted like heroes, much the way they'd been greeted in Berat. They sat through speeches and dined on grapes and cheese. Unlike their stay in Berat, however, this time they moved on after one night.

Leaving Përmet, they continued climbing Mount Nemërçkë, a steep, difficult mountain that Duffy believed would be the path with the least German and Ballista activity. The climb was difficult and cold, but at least there was no blizzard to endure this time.

Upon reaching the peak of Nemërçkë, the party hiked about three hours down the other side until they reached the village of Sheper. Here they met another SOE officer, Major Harold William "Bill" Tilman, who made his headquarters in the settlement. Tilman was a decorated veteran of World War I (1914–1918) and a world-famous mountain climber. He had been part of three expeditions up Mount Everest.

Tilman provided the Americans with tea and Western magazines. His radio pulled in some jazz music, and the men and women were able to relax for a while.

Duffy met with Tilman, Thrasher and Baggs to plan their route to the sea. Tilman told them that he was expecting a shipment of supplies in a couple of days, and he suggested they wait. But Duffy was eager to move on. He told the Americans they would be hiking about 40 kilometres the next day, their longest trek yet.

· · · · ·

Meanwhile, the American officer Lloyd Smith had waited in his seaside cave for five days without getting any word of the Americans. The cave was cold and infested with lice from the goats and sheep that used to live there. Smith was eager to get out of there, so finally he set out to find Tilman at a village called Kuç. He'd heard Tilman might know something.

Accompanied by a shepherd as a guide, he hiked to the village of Dukat, which was occupied by Ballista soldiers. There he learned of fighting in the area and that Germans occupied the town between there and Kuç. Smith insisted on going forward anyway, and his guide fled the scene. The Ballista offered to send three of their own soldiers with Smith if he promised to bring them back safely. Smith agreed, and he and the Ballista guides set out.

After a few hours, they ran into a group of heavily armed partisans on the trail. This made the Ballista with Smith quite nervous – even more so when one of the partisans accompanied them as they continued. But, determined to find the Americans, or at least information about them, Smith used all his wits – and bribing money – to smooth things over and get to Tilman.

When the group arrived in Tërbac, the village that the Ballista said was occupied by Germans, they found more partisans instead. After Smith and the partisans chatted a bit about the progress of the war, the partisans told him that they were taking his three Ballista guides prisoner. Smith refused. He threatened the weight of the US government would come down on their heads if they took his guides, thus blocking his mission.

At that, the partisans relented. They suggested he head to another village, Ramicë, where their commandant was stationed, so Smith hiked that way followed by 10 of the partisans. When he met the commandant, he had no information about the Americans. Undeterred, Smith decided to head back to Seaview and see if any new information had come in over the radio. He made his way back, first stopping in Tërbaç where the partisans had been stationed.

Beyond the village, the partisans were fighting some German soldiers on the road. Not wanting to walk into a firefight, Smith decided to camp in town. Later, partisans came back to town loaded down with German boots, rifles, pistols and a machine gun. Apparently it had been a successful battle for the partisans.

The next morning, the partisans again tried to take Smith's Ballista guides prisoner. He was arguing for their release when German soldiers suddenly

approached the town. The guides were released, and

they headed back where they'd come from with Smith.

In spite of Smith's determination, it was a wasted trip.

He had learned nothing new about the stranded

American medics and nurses.

CHAPTER 11

GERMAN AVALANCHE

The morning of 15 December, the group set out on their 40-kilometre trip to the town of Gjirokastër. For more than four hours, they walked briskly along a river, stopping to rest in the late afternoon. While they sat overlooking a wide, flat field that, according to Duffy, had once been used by the Italians as an airfield, one of the Americans came up with an idea. Why not have a plane fly in and rescue them?

No, Duffy said – and little more. His response frustrated the Americans. They certainly trusted Duffy, who was extremely competent and experienced, but they couldn't understand why an air rescue wouldn't work. They would find out soon enough.

By about 6.00 that evening, they'd crossed the field, and Gjirokastër was just ahead. But before they could go any farther, Duffy signalled for everyone to get down. They took cover in the woods, and he scanned the distance to examine a pair of headlights moving along the road in the dusk. The car continued on and faded from sight, but Duffy waited until it was dark before moving the group along.

Gjirokastër was a hillside town of about 12,000 people with a large castle at the top. It was the birthplace of General Hoxha. A schoolhouse there served as partisan headquarters. They went inside the schoolhouse and met with some partisan leaders who talked with Duffy under a dim light bulb. Then the Americans were divided into smaller groups and put up in homes for the night.

The evening had some pleasant surprises for certain members of the group. The home where Jensen was staying had an indoor toilet. Hayes and some of the other medics stayed in a home with a man called Haki, who got oranges for the men. It was the first fruit they'd had since the small bits of quince they tasted after leaving Berat many weeks ago. To some it felt as though their luck may be turning good again.

While the Americans were settling in, Duffy and his radioman, Bell, decoded messages from SOE headquarters in Egypt. They learned that Germans were moving in the same direction they were – towards Seaview. They should continue with their journey cautiously. Duffy was disturbed by all the Nazi activity, but he was pleased that they could keep moving.

· · · · ·

The next few days, the weather was bitterly cold.

Adding to the bleakness, the towns they came across

were ravaged by war – buildings burned down, food

stores withered away to nearly nothing. They came

across many locals on the trail, fleeing from the fighting.

They were bloody and terrified. Some carried a few

belongings or small children. The badly injured were

carried on makeshift stretchers. All the refugees as well

as the Nazi presence was unnerving to the Americans

and Duffy, Bell and Steffa. Everyone's mood grew dim.

Tempers got short.

Again, the Americans asked Duffy about an air

rescue. A plane could easily land on that old Italian

airstrip, they pressed.

But Duffy gave them an icy look and explained it was too dangerous. For one thing, the enemy might be intercepting their radio communication. If they arranged such a thing, they might be ambushed. For another, an escape like that would surely get the Nazis' attention, and they'd make all the locals in the area pay for helping them get away.

The group reached the village of Progonat on 17 December. Pandee talked with some of the village elders, and he reported to the rest of the group what he found out. Intense fighting was happening on the route they intended to take. Dead Albanians lay all over the place. For their own safety, there was no choice but to turn around.

Of all the tough news and obstacles the nurses and medics had encountered on their long journey, this may have been the hardest to take. They knew that they were a mere two-day walk away from the coast. They were so close to freedom, but now they'd have to turn and head back inland.

"We were washed up," Abbott later wrote. They had climbed mountains on their hands and knees, lived on sour milk and cornbread, slept with lice and fleas, and more. All these things they could do because they believed there was hope. The sea was nearby, and they would make it. But now, as Abbott surveyed the group, he saw that they had lost that hope. "We'd made a good fight of it," he wrote, "but the fight was over."

They contemplated surrendering to the Germans. At least that would end their savage journey. Instead, they hiked eastwards. It was lucky they did, because the Germans stormed through the area in force. In his report, Duffy said, "The German drive was an avalanche."

· · · · ·

By this point, the Americans had been trapped in Albania for six weeks. Thrasher and Baggs approached Duffy once more about requesting an aeroplane rescue. Again, Duffy denied the request.

Tersely, Duffy explained that he had orders to take the Americans to the coast. He was not going to fail in that directive. But he did allow Thrasher to try to contact his own air force – the Americans.

"Well, okay," Baggs said.

"We'll take responsibility for this," Thrasher added.

"You're damn right you will," Duffy snapped.

Thrasher had the radioman Bell send a message to the commanding officer of the Twelfth US Army. The path to the coast was completely overrun by Nazis, the message said, and the party was exhausted, hungry, cold and many were ill. He requested a C-47 to pick them up at the airfield by Gjirokastër. He said he could ensure that no enemy aircraft was in the area, and they'd be protected by partisan fighters on the ground.

The SOE at Cairo received the message and forwarded it to the American Army Air Forces, adding that they were asking for Duffy's opinion on an air evacuation.

An ice storm struck as the stranded Americans marched, wet and miserable, into Kolonja. They were given places to stay for a couple of nights. Locals stood guard while the Americans slept, watching for Germans or Ballists. On the second morning, the villagers ejected the group from their village with great haste.

Duffy's new course was towards the village of Doksat, which was about 1.5 kilometres away from Gjirokastër and very near the airfield. The group set out to their new destination facing bitter sheets of sleet. As before, they met hundreds of refugees along the way, and there among one of the crowds they were charmed to find their old friend Hasan Gina. The once moustached but now clean-shaven commandant had taken them in after their plane crashed. He had protected them and led them to Berat. He hugged Baggs and shook many of the Americans' hands.

They talked for a while, and then Hasan asked where Ann Maness was. He made a motion to indicate her long hair. Jensen told him she was still trapped back in Berat with two other nurses. Hasan swore to kill extra Germans to get revenge.

Duffy found homes for the Americans to stay in that night in a small village called Karla, where Hasan was also staying. But when Jensen sought Hasan out to talk again in the morning, she was disappointed to find that he had disappeared again. She and the other Americans considered him a friend and had been happy to see him.

After a long hike the next day, the group had to cross a road that the Germans had begun using regularly. They waited until the dark of night, when it happened to be raining, and then Duffy sent them scurrying across one at a time. They were instructed to keep going into the woods until they reached a riverbank. There they would be ferried across the river in groups.

As they ran across the road and down to the riverbank, they couldn't see much of anything in the dark night. The boat appeared out of the blackness – a rickety-looking vessel – but it got them all across safely. On the far side, they were directed up the trail to a house. When they'd all made it, they were served a meal of boiled potatoes, the first solid meal they'd had in days.

It was no time to relax, though. Duffy felt the house was too close to the road, so after they'd eaten, they continued walking for a couple more hours before taking refuge in another village.

· · · · ·

During this time, the American Captain Smith was also moving through the landscape to avoid Germans. He made it to the outskirts of Dukat. It was the village where he had picked up the three Ballista guides and returned them safely home as promised. There he learned that Germans now occupied the town, but some villagers helped him get through by disguising him as a shepherd. Then he walked in plain sight through the middle of town without being discovered, though his nerves were quite on edge.

Smith made it back to the Seaview camp the next day. But when he heard that the Americans were heading towards Kuç, he left again right away.

On 22 December, while staying in Dhermi, Smith learned that the Germans were coming into villages and searching homes for partisans and weapons. When the Germans came to Dhermi, he escaped and took refuge in a cave, where he spent the night with a shepherd and his flock.

On 23 December, the medics and nurses approached Doksat. Thrasher and Baggs took time to inspect the airfield, making sure it was smooth and long enough for a C-47 to land. They also inspected for evidence of mines. Everything appeared satisfactory.

Doksat was a pleasant town with stone streets. So far it had not been hit by the Germans. Tilman, the famous mountaineer, was there to greet the party, as was another

SOE officer, a radio operator called Willie Williamson. All the British officers stayed together in a stone house, and the pilots and nurses were divided among other homes in the town. The medics hiked about 15 minutes farther up the trail to stay in another village.

When Jensen and two other nurses entered the home where they were to stay the night, she noticed right away that something was different. The fireplace had a chimney, so no smoke filled the room. Even nicer, the couple who lived there produced a fresh orange for each of the women. They ate the juicy treats slowly to savour them.

CHAPTER 12

CHRISTMAS AND A NEAR RESCUE

Over the past few days, people in the party had been bickering among themselves. Nerves were frayed, and they were all mentally and physically exhausted. They needed rest, including Duffy. He told them that they'd stay in Doksat for a few days to recuperate. What he didn't tell them was that he'd chosen this location because of its closeness to the airfield. He was still against trying an aeroplane rescue, but if the American Army Air Forces came through, he wanted to bc ready.

The next day was Christmas Eve. For the medics

in the next town over, the day started out promisingly

as the cook in their house produced a beef carcass

and began to cook it. They looked forward to a proper

Christmas dinner with great excitement. While they

waited, they noticed many partisan soldiers coming in

and out of the kitchen. They didn't think much about

it, and when dinner was served, the men stood around

the table in quiet gratitude. One of the men asked

Abbott to say a prayer – they knew he always carried a

small prayer book in his pocket. Abbott read a blessing,

and they sat down to eat. But the cook only gave them

each a meagre helping of scraps. Where was all that

meat, they wondered.

The soldiers had eaten most of it, the cook told them.

Disappointed and frustrated, the medics ate what

was given to them. They made the best of the night by

singing a few Christmas carols and telling stories about home. "Silent night! Holy night!" they sang. "All is calm! All is bright." Abbott was overcome with emotion and began to weep.

As usual, their luck was fickle. This time, it was the luck of the draw, because over in Doksat, the nurses, the pilots and the Brits were having a more robust Christmas Eve celebration. Markowitz, Jensen and Schwant left the house where they were staying and walked down the street, stopping at the pilots' house. Jensen wasn't sure she wanted to celebrate with everyone because they had been bickering so much recently. Everyone was frustrated with the lousy weather and slow progress, scared of the Nazi presence, exhausted and hungry. It might be best to be alone, she thought.

When she went inside, the room was dim. The other nurses as well as the pilots and the British officers were there. On the table in the corner of the room was a cedar branch decorated with a few small red bows. The simple decoration seemed like one of the most beautiful things Jensen had ever seen.

"Wherever did you get decorations?" she asked.

The other nurses had found the bough, and one of them had produced some ribbon from her bag. The group sang a few Christmas carols. It turned out Steffa knew more of the words than any of the Americans. He'd learned them at his Albanian-American school as a boy. In addition to Christmas carols, they also sang "God Save the King" and "The Star-Spangled Banner". Jensen was glad she came after all. It was a nice reminder that they were all in this together, and everyone appreciated the opportunity to relax and be joyful.

The next morning, on Christmas Day, Jensen went to church with her host family, who had invited her. They were honoured to have the American guest accompany them. Though it was at 5.00 in the morning, and she didn't understand any of the service because it was in Greek and Albanian, it must have felt like a small bit of normal life injected into her adventure. Afterwards, as she walked back to the house with her hosts, she saw the first streaks of dawn brighten the sky.

· · · · ·

That afternoon, the entire party gathered in Duffy's assigned house to celebrate Christmas. They ate a chicken dinner and made toasts to Christmas and to "the coast". The hostess danced a Tosk, which some of the American women tried too. While they all laughed and had some fun for once, all were thinking about their families back home. For some of the medics, a few of whom were only teenagers, it was their first Christmas away. They told stories of their home lives, and then their thoughts turned again to the three missing nurses – Porter, Maness and Lytle. The Americans asked Duffy what he thought had happened to them.

He admitted he didn't know, but he said if they'd been captured, he would have heard about it. It was just as well, he said. And he advised everyone not to ask or talk about them. The Germans probably assumed that all of them were together, but if they got wind that there were three others splintered off, they'd certainly search them out.

• • • • •

Back in Bari, Italy, plans for the air rescue were underway, much to the concern of the British. The Americans were taking control of the operation, under the direct orders of President Franklin Delano Roosevelt. FDR was tired of waiting for the Brits to extract the Americans, especially the nurses, whom he called the "flower of American womanhood", from danger. So the air rescue was sped up in spite of British protests.

Duffy's reports of heavy German presence did not deter the Americans from sending in a plane. Neither did the fact that it was assumed the Nazis had spies in Bari who probably had heard of the plans. And neither did the fact that the airstrip lay in a valley that would be easy for the enemy to shell with artillery. As far as FDR was concerned, the biggest risk was to keep waiting for something else to happen. After all, Duffy had been leading the Americans all over Albania for nearly a month, and they were still not at the coast.

Furthermore, by this time the American officer Lloyd Smith had been in the country for nearly three weeks. He'd been dodging Nazis that whole time, and he was no closer to reaching the stranded Americans. Smith was ordered back to Italy.

• • • • •

A day or two after Christmas, a huge group of Germans began to fill up the nearby town of Gjirokastër. From motorcycles to tanks, vehicles of all sizes moved down the street. Duffy watched them through binoculars from the top floor of a house in Doksat. Among the equipment being loaded was anti-aircraft guns, which clearly was bad news for any air rescue. Gjirokastër was about as close to the airfield as Doksat.

A couple of days earlier, a car full of German officers had been killed, Duffy noted. The increased German presence was probably payback. The nurses guessed it was Hasan Gina who'd killed the Germans, fulfilling his promise. How would he have known it would backfire on them like this?

Duffy sent word to Jon Naar, the intelligence officer who was coordinating the rescue, that the aeroplane rescue should be cancelled. It would be a disaster. But due to the bad weather, his message didn't get through to Cairo where Naar was.

For the time being, it didn't matter because the weather was too rainy and foggy to attempt a landing anyway. So the party stayed put in Doksat, taking turns looking through binoculars at the Germans in the neighbouring town and waiting.

AND WAITING.

Finally, on 28 December, word got to Duffy that the following day a C-47 would be landing on the airfield. It would be escorted by fighter planes for cover. Duffy revealed the plan to the Americans, who were stunned.

For his part, Duffy was not excited about the manoeuvre. With all that artillery next door, it seemed reckless. But the medics and nurses were overwhelmed with joy. They were sick, malnourished, infested with lice and injured. They had been shot at. They had climbed thousands of vertical metres, trudged through snow as high as their waists and been hunted like game. They were tired and weak. But now, at last, it seemed that their long, terrible journey was about to end.

"We'd never been so happy," Abbott wrote. "That was it. We wanted to pinch ourselves to make sure it was no dream."

On the morning of the 29th, the party gathered to hear Duffy's plan for getting them on the plane. With the radio still not working to send messages, they would have to communicate with the pilots another way. If it was safe to land, Duffy said, they would make a large X on the field with yellow parachute panels to indicate as much to the pilots. If not, they would simply stay hidden and the planes would pass by.

At the appointed time later that morning, the Americans gathered with Steffa and Bell at a hill near the airfield. The medics who had volunteered to pull out the signal gripped their pieces of parachute nervously. Sick and sore but very excited, they all waited to hear the planes. Instead, they heard motors rumbling nearby on the ground. Duffy noticed three German trucks and one armoured car driving down from Gjirokastër and parking on the road in front of the airfield. This was too much, Duffy decided. Any chance they had of pulling off the daring air rescue was gone now. A cold wind cut into him and the others. He did not put out the safe signal.

Then they heard the aeroplanes – more than any of them had imagined would come. An earthquake of a rumble filled the sky as more than 20 Lockheed P-38 Lightning fighters, one British Wellington bomber and two C-47s flew towards them. The Americans didn't know it, but another nine fighters had flown to the airfield near Berat where the group had crashed so long ago. Their job was to strafe the field to prevent enemy aircraft from taking off. The other fighters were there to protect the bomber and the two transports.

The fighters flew patterns in the sky. The C-47s swooped as low as 15 metres over the ground. The noise was deafening. The incredible display of power was awe-inspiring. The nurses and medics were devastated. It was hard to take – all that hardware sent over by both the United States and Britain, and the Americans could do nothing but watch, hidden.

Duffy later said it was the hardest decision he'd ever made, but he still refused to put out the signal. As the planes made a third pass over the field, he looked around at the nurses. Some of them were crying.

"Just imagine the feeling," Duffy later wrote, "seeing the transports make three passes at the field, so near yet so far – it almost seemed you could touch the planes, they were so low. The nurses had unquestionably suffered a very hard time – this was indeed too much."

But at the last second, Duffy changed his mind. The more he thought about it, with all that firepower in the air, they could probably make the escape. He yelled to the medics with the parachutes to start running down the hill. They didn't have time to make the proper signal, but maybe the pilots would notice the brightly coloured parachutes. However, just as the men began running down, a couple of the fighter planes fired on the German trucks on the road, and then they all flew away. They'd given up.

The men stopped at the edge of the field, which was a lucky thing. With the armed Germans sitting just off another side, the party would have been sitting ducks. "The Germans could have rounded us up then as easy as picking sweet corn in August," Abbott later wrote.

As the medics went back up the hill, they found their American friends crying and demoralized. But strangely, although the rescue had failed, the group felt emboldened to know that so much effort had been put in on their behalf. So many people – from the locals in Albania to the British SOE officers and the pilots who'd just flown over – had risked their lives to help them get home safely. The Americans felt that they owed it to all these people to make it home now. Although they were devastated by the setback, they were more determined than ever.

CHAPTER 13

HIKING BY NIGHT

In the base at Seaview, Captain Smith was
still waiting for his boat to take him back to Italy.
Conditions there were miserable and getting worse.
It was cold and unsanitary, and their food supply was
low. One of the officers there had died of pneumonia.
One, Major Jerry Field, had an explosive go off in his
face. He fell from the cave and bounced off the rocks,
suffering broken bones and a detached eyeball. The
others in the base put his eyeball back in with a spoon.

Smith must have been eager to get out of there and head back to Italy. However, when the next boat arrived, it brought new officers and a new message for Smith – stay there. The Germans had cleared out from most of the villages in which they'd been, and his path was once again clear to reach the Americans. He did not know about the attempted air rescue, only that his mission of finding the stranded party was back on.

· · · · ·

Duffy had been told that the aeroplanes might try again, so the party hung around Doksat for a few days, keeping a close eye on the Germans in the next town. The villagers were eager for them to leave – they were low on food and nervous about the possibility that Germans would discover them. When Hornsby and Abbott, on watch in the woods, discovered that the Germans were questioning locals about going to Doksat, they reported the news to Duffy. Duffy immediately got the party on the move to Saraqinishtë, where they were once again settled in small groups into houses. The night they arrived, it was New Year's Eve.

Two days later, Duffy announced that he'd cancelled the air evacuation. It was getting harder to track the German movements, and the weather had not got better. In fact, the rain had turned to snow. Besides that, their path to the coast appeared to be opening up. He planned to stay in Saraqinishtë long enough to get a fresh shipment of supplies that Tilman had received in Sheper. Duffy had also learned that the American Captain Smith was working his way towards them.

When Tilman's supplies arrived, they included new shirts for the men and fresh boots for several of them.

The men even got to take baths before putting on the new clothing. "We felt like a million bucks," Abbott wrote.

Duffy checked in with Jensen about everyone's condition. Was the group ready for some harsh travels? Jensen thought so. They had some issues to worry about, including Shumway's knee, but the dysentery was finally starting to fade. She pronounced the group ready and eager to go. Duffy was delighted with the news.

When they left Saraqinishtë on 4 January, they hiked with renewed energy. They had eaten well while in the village. Duffy had purchased mules to carry equipment. They walked so quickly that they arrived at the next village ahead of schedule. Instead of pushing on, Duffy told them to lay low in houses until the sun went down. His messengers had reported lots of German activity in the area, and he wanted to hike at night. They had a small meal and left town at sundown.

A cold, vicious rain came down as they hiked. Duffy told them not to talk, use torches, or even smoke on the trail. Any small hint could give away their presence to the enemy. When they arrived at a river a couple of hours later, the rain had let up, but they were all drenched and shivering. Abbott noticed that it was deathly quiet. The moon provided a little light from behind the clouds. It was the same river they'd crossed on their way to Doksat before Christmas.

They crossed the river and approached the enemy's patrolled road on the other side. Duffy told the group that they would cross together – and very quickly. Abbott recalled the field they crossed with Hasan so many weeks ago. It was a similar situation, crossing an open area with no cover and Germans all around. They had been lucky that time, Abbott thought. They'd been lucky so many times. Could their luck possibly hold?

They crossed the road with no incident and made it to a battle-wrecked village called Midhar. The women stayed there, while the medics were taken by guide to another town an hour away.

· · · · ·

Nobody slept well that night, and everyone woke up early ready to get back on the trail. In spite of their aches, hunger and exhaustion, all were motivated by the idea of making it to the coast. The beginning of the day's hike was highlighted by a severe thunderstorm. Later, the rain turned to sleet, and finally to hail. They bunked that night in Golem, a town they'd been in twice already, which caused some grumbling among the gang.

The next morning, moving through a snowstorm, they scaled a slush-covered mountain. Their guide made a wrong turn, which cost them extra hours in the blizzard. The snow fell so hard that they couldn't see their hands in front of their faces. They couldn't hear each other without yelling. When nurse Tacina's mule stumbled, she fell off and tumbled down a ravine. Duffy dived after her, and they both emerged covered in snow but unharmed.

After emerging from the second blizzard of their Albanian ordeal, they had to cross a stream by jumping from stone to stone. Eldridge slipped and got back up soaked to the bone and shivering. Nurse Dawson also slipped. Duffy tried to catch her, and they both ended up in water over their knees.

"He was so mad you could almost see his clothes steaming," Abbott wrote about Duffy.

About 3.00 that afternoon, they arrived in Kuç, and Duffy immediately began asking about Captain Smith.

Nobody had seen him, but half an hour later he walked into the village.

· · · · ·

Though Smith was limping on a cane – he'd been injured somehow – he looked strong and imposing. The American had blond hair, a blond beard and wore a British military coat.

Many in the party had not even known that an American officer had been dispatched to help them. So meeting Captain Smith sent a jolt of confidence through the group, which had just suffered through a miserable few days.

They left the village around 9.00 the next morning, frost on the ground, their breath puffing out in clouds. One of their mules kept falling and dislodging the gear it was carrying, but they reached Tërbaç, their destination for the day, in the afternoon. Little was left of this village, which had been decimated by the Germans. The room where Hayes and his group were bunked had a big hole in the wall.

With little shelter and no blankets or food, Smith suggested that they press on. The British officers opposed this idea, but they agreed to let the group decide. Smith gathered the party and told them his idea. If they left now, they would walk until dawn. They were heading into Ballista territory. But for the Americans it was no choice at all. None of them liked the idea of waiting any more when they were so close to the sea. Although everyone needed rest, they voted to press forward now. Smith was surprised and impressed by their energy.

Before they could leave, they had to hire new mule drivers. The muleteers they'd been using thus far refused to go any farther due to the Ballista presence in the area. Smith threatened one of the mule drivers with his pistol in order to keep the mules themselves. He found others in the town willing to actually drive the mules. In returning the Ballista guides safely home a few weeks ago, Smith had earned a good reputation. The new mule drivers trusted him.

They left town walking as quickly as they could muster in the snow. Smith and a guide raced ahead even more quickly in order to make sure the path and upcoming villages were indeed free of Nazi threats. When they reached the peak of the mountain at about 11.00 that night, Steffa announced that it was time for him to turn back. The mountain peak was the dividing line between Ballista and partisan territory, and it was for Steffa's safety that he turned back.

The nurses and medics were sad to see him go. They had been with him for a long time, and he had done so much for them. They were especially regretful that they had doubted his loyalty early on. Jensen gave him the flight pin off her uniform and told him to give it to his son, who had admired it when they first met. Steffa told her that he had brothers in Ohio, USA. He asked her to contact them when she got home and let them know that he and his family were okay.

The group caught up to Smith and his guide in Dukat, where Smith had paid the Ballists for food and safe passage. Smith allowed the partisan guides to return home, and the nurses were taken into the nicest home they'd seen in Albania, where they were served hot tea with sugar. They ate cornbread, goats' cheese and sweet pastries. They didn't know it, but they were probably in the home of a powerful Ballista chieftain.

They had just finished their snack when Smith pulled up in an old Italian truck and told everyone to get on board. The truck had an open bed with side rails but no canopy. As they climbed on, Smith gave them stern instructions. They were heading into heavily occupied territory. If they ran into Germans, the truck would stop and everyone was to jump off and hide away from the road. The truck would continue on and come back for them later, when it was safer. The British were all armed with machine guns. If they had to use them, Smith said, the Americans were to hit the ground and stay down. Smith promised they'd eliminate the enemy quickly.

After weeks of walking, the truck would save them hours. Everyone settled into the crowded truck bed and they all hoped they wouldn't be stopped. It wasn't long, though, before a headlight was spotted and the truck stopped. The passengers piled out and hid off the road as a

German motorcycle rode past. They crammed back in and drove for a while longer until another vehicle was spotted. It was a truck with its lights off. As their truck stopped, the other truck stopped ahead of them. The two vehicles faced each other on the dark road. Smith told the Americans to be still and wait. If the other truck's headlights came on, they should scatter into the woods.

Smith sent his driver to talk to whoever was in the other truck – Nazis, they presumed. The driver trembled with fear, and the medics and nurses did the same. Abbott noted that he would not have traded places with that driver for anything. When the other truck's lights ignited the road, the Americans ran for their lives. It turned out that the other truck had been stolen by partisans. Soon the crew was back on the road and safely inside a stone farmhouse making preparations for the final leg of their journey.

CHAPTER 14

TO THE SEA – AND ACROSS

Their safe house for the night was a stone farmhouse owned by an English-speaking Albanian who had helped the SOE set up the base at Seaview. Xhelil Çela was a well-trusted ally.

They only rested a short time at the house, though, before Smith pushed them on. His goal was to reach the peak of Dukati Mountain before sunrise so the enemy wouldn't see them from the road. From there, they'd go down the other side to the sea. It was a steep climb, and Smith and Duffy ordered many rests, but the Americans urged them on each time. They were tired of taking little breaks. They were ready for a long rest. They had had enough.

Around 9.00 in the morning, they reached the top of Dukati Mountain and looked down the other side. The Adriatic Sea glistened in the morning sun.

"Sight of it almost overpowered us for a minute," Abbott wrote. "We simply stood and stared at that patch of open water."

"We made it!" Jensen said. "I knew we could. I just knew we'd make it!"

They hadn't actually made it yet. They still had to get down the side of the mountain while sneaking past enemy lairs and watching out for patrols. But energy and morale were high, and the group surged forward. They didn't run into any enemies. By the afternoon, they'd reached the bottom of the mountain, where they were greeted by SOE officers from Seaview. The officers brought chocolate, which the party gobbled up in celebration of making it thus far.

The group made their way towards Seaview. This final stretch was a struggle. They'd slept no more than eight hours out of the last 96, and they were severely fatigued. At one point, Jensen and Watson both buckled and fell. Their friends picked them up and helped them continue on. This was no time to let their determination lag.

Finally, they reached the caves of Seaview. The British officers radioed to Bari that the group was ready for the boat. Bari radioed back – the boat would be there around midnight that night. The Americans collapsed in various spots in the caves to sleep.

• • • • •

The rescue boat, aptly named *The Yankee*, left Bari around 2.00 p.m. The crew motored across the sea trying to pick up radio communication from Seaview.

At about 10.30 that night, British Lieutenant Commander "Sandy" Glen woke everyone up. It was time to get down by the water. "No lights, no smoking and keep your talk low," Smith told them. The party climbed down the trail to the shore while American Corporal Don Orahood waved the antenna of his radio in the air trying to find the best reception. Finally he reached *The Yankee*. "They're out there!" he said.

The group stood on a small patch of sand, all straining their eyes in the dark, hoping to see the boat. Suddenly, a rubber raft emerged from the darkness. Abbott felt his heart leap. In groups of four or five at a time, the crew of the raft took the Americans out to *The Yankee*, which was anchored away from shore in the dark.

When all were aboard, the boat lurched forward, and they were on their way across the sea. No one turned to say goodbye to Albania.

The ship ran into rough water along the way, and many of the nurses and medics became violently seasick. Some of them, though, including Ann Markowitz, counted it a pleasure to throw up in a real toilet after weeks of puking in the woods.

The crew told them that there was a naval battle occurring between Allied and German boats, and they had to navigate around that, adding some time to their journey. No matter. The Americans were on their way to the comfort and safety of Allied territory.

The group of exhausted medics, nurses and flight crew arrived in Bari at about 1.30 in the afternoon on 9 January. Their plane had crash-landed in that Albanian field 63 days ago. Now, as they docked, they saw their commanding officer, Major William McKnight, beaming from the dock. He was surrounded by dozens of photographers and others who were eager to greet the returning heroes. Also among them was Jon Naar, the intelligence officer, and other SOE officers, waiting to greet their colleagues.

Before they got off the boat, all of the medics and nurses thanked Duffy, Bell and Smith for all they had done to help save them. It had been an emotional journey, and no matter how determined or lucky the Americans had been, they never could have got away without the help of these brave officers.

• • • • •

Back on 2 December, the Nazis had bombed the port of Bari in an attack some were calling a "Little Pearl

Harbor". One hundred and five German Junkers Ju 88

bombers had taken the town completely by surprise

and bombed 27 ships, including two ammunition ships.

These ships had exploded, causing damage up to 11

kilometres away. A fuel pipeline was burst open, and

gushing fuel caught fire, sending sheets of flame over the

harbour and ships. One ship, which had been carrying a

secret cargo of mustard gas bombs, was also destroyed.

Mustard gas leaked into the waters. More than 600

people suffered blindness and chemical burns from the

spill. At least 1,000 people were killed.

In addition, much of the hospital equipment – which

had been on board a ship in the harbour – had sunk. The

hospital itself had been wrecked and rebuilt. It had only

been open for two days when the medics and nurses of the

807th were taken there. Even the beds had been borrowed.

The American medics and nurses, freshly escaped from

Albania, were the hospital's first patients. They got warm baths and clean pyjamas and slippers. Jensen stayed in bed while her twisted intestinal system sorted itself out again.

Thrasher and Baggs were taken away for separate questioning by intelligence officers. The medics and nurses never saw them again. The rest of them would be questioned too. In fact, when the major who interrogated Jensen saw her notes, he confiscated them. He told her she could get them back after the war, which she did.

After the questioning was finished, the officers who had interviewed them produced a map of the journey that they'd made from the interviews. It showed that the crash site was about 97 kilometres from Seaview, but the route they took covered about 547 kilometres. With all the climbing up and down mountains, the officer calculated that the group had walked between 1,046 and 1,609 kilometres.

All of them were warned not to talk about the specifics of their ordeal to anyone, and they were all forced to sign agreements promising they wouldn't. A writer from the Associated Press wrote about their story, but he was given false information, and the British involvement was ignored. The Allies didn't want the enemy to learn just how much help the partisans had been or just how strong the SOE was in the area. Also, if any names of towns or people leaked out, the Germans would surely find them and take revenge on them.

By 26 January nearly all of the rescued Americans were healthy enough to travel home to see their families in the United States. Most of them would never see one another again.

CHAPTER 15

SAVING THE FINAL THREE

In spite of the celebrating, the business of rescuing American nurses from Albania was not yet finished. Ann Maness, Helen Porter and Wilma Lytle still remained in that farmhouse in Berat, hiding and waiting.

Over the two months, the nurses had stayed hidden inside the farmhouse. Several British officers still in Albania made a first attempt to reach the nurses by foot, but they were ambushed by Ballista. The would-be British heroes, including Victor Smith, who had met the other 27 nurses back in December, were lucky to escape.

They turned back to their base in Krushovë.

Again, the SOE and its American counterpart, the OSS, worked together on a new plan. The American Lloyd Smith was sent back to Seaview to put the plan in place. He arrived in Seaview the night of 2 February. The new plan involved giving cloth to the nurses and getting them to sew clothing that would disguise them as local civilians. Then Albanian guides would take them by car to the mountains where Smith would escort them over the mountain to Seaview. There, they would take a boat to Bari, just as the others had.

Smith was teamed up with SOE Major Anthony Quayle and an American civilian Dale "Tank" McAdoo, who was working with the OSS. His radioman was Nick Kukich, a Marine sergeant from Ohio. They gathered at Sea Elephant, another base the Allies held on the coast of Albania. Probably the most important weapon they had was the supply of money with which Smith had been armed. He would use it to bribe local leaders and fighters along their journey.

The Albanian of critical importance was Tare Shyti, a regional leader who was not aligned with the Ballists or the partisans. When he was young, Shyti's father had been murdered. At the age of 11, Shyti killed his father's killer, thus gaining the enduring respect of everyone in his region of Albania. His family was well connected through business as well. He was known as a man who could get things done. Smith thought that he was just the man to spearhead the daring rescue of the three remaining nurses. He used his ample gold to buy Shyti's help.

Shyti headed inland to obtain false documents for the trapped nurses. The papers would identify the nurses as Albanians. He then brought them to the women in Berat.

Smith sent a message to the Albanian government leader, Midhat Fasheri, alerting him to the plan and letting him know that if the nurses didn't make it out alive, he would blame the Ballista. The Allies would surely retaliate. Fasheri agreed to help facilitate the escape under the noses of the Germans.

Meanwhile, Nazis were beginning to patrol near the coastal bases. Smith sent scouts disguised as shepherds to keep an eye on their movements. He didn't want the nurses to make it all the way here only to run into a nest of German troops. When German patrols got too close, Seaview and Sea Elephant were evacuated, and everyone split up. Smith and Kukich hiked up a snowy mountain and waited out a cold night under a thin blanket. They later met up with the rest of their crew at Dukat.

· · · · ·

For Maness, Lytle and Porter, the days and weeks piled up with no word from the outside world. The Ballista commandant in Berat, Kadre Çakrani, continued to visit them and update them on what was going on. In January, he came with the news that the rest of their party had escaped Albania. The nurses grew restless and began to talk about making their own escape by foot.

Finally, in early March, Çakrani came to them with good news – a plan for their escape had begun. Goni went into town to buy materials for the dresses and head scarves and helped them sew the clothing.

Shyti and another man visited the nurses next. Tomorrow, the men said, they'd return to take the nurses' pictures for the fake IDs. Arranging for these papers was the main reason things had taken so long. It was now the middle of March. Lloyd Smith had commissioned Shyti to get the fake papers back on 3 February.

The extra time was worth it, though. The papers had new names for the nurses and included all the official stamps. These documents would withstand scrutiny.

On 18 March Shyti arrived again with his cousin, Meço. The three nurses used a secret passageway that connected Goni's house to a neighbouring house, where a truck, a car and several Ballista soldiers waited for them. The women got into the car. Maness was in the passenger seat with a rifle between her knees. Shyti, along with the Ballista soldiers and the women's personal belongings, were piled into the truck.

They had the opportunity to test their disguises almost right away. The car got a flat tyre, and while the driver repaired it, several Germans came past. The nurses had been taught to look down in the presence of the enemy, which was not only how local women would act but also helped to hide the blue eyes of Porter and Lytle – which would have been a dead giveaway. The Germans didn't give them a second look.

The group was stopped a few times, but they were always allowed to pass through. When they reached Vlorë, a port city that marked the end of the driving portion of their journey, a Nazi read their papers while Maness and the others waited, their nerves on edge. The guard waved them on, and shortly after that the group hiked up a trail, crossed a stream and walked farther until they reached the safe house that was their destination for the night.

The next morning, Lloyd Smith – who had been hiding out in a shepherd's hut – was alerted that the nurses had made it. He met them on the trail and brought them back to the hut, where they spent the day in hiding, waiting for nightfall. When dark arrived, Smith led the group to the stone farmhouse of Xhelil Çela, the same house where the other nurses and medics had stopped before climbing the mountain and reaching the sea. It was a reliable safe house for the OSS and SOE.

Well after midnight, Smith announced that it was time to go. They had to crest the mountain before daylight to avoid being seen by Germans on the road. Like the other Americans before them, the nurses were energized and up to the task. They hiked all night and into the morning, reaching the top of the mountain, climbing down the other side, and sneaking their way to the caves at Seaview in the early afternoon.

Kukich radioed to Bari that the nurses had arrived. The nurses waited for nearly two days for the weather to clear up. Finally, at nearly midnight on 21 March, an Italian motorboat driven by an OSS operative appeared in the gloomy night to pick them up. They'd been in Albania for 135 days.

The sea was rough. It took them about 13 hours to make it across the Adriatic Sea. The nurses suffered from severe seasickness. When they arrived in Otranto, Italy, the following afternoon, no press or photographers were waiting for them. There was no party. They were taken by ambulance up to the hospital in Bari and released a short time later. At last, against remarkable odds, all of the nurses and medics, and all four of the flight crew, had escaped from Albania.

• • • • •

By late 1944, the partisans and Allies had taken control of Albania to such an extent that the Germans fled the country. The partisans who had helped the Americans with their escape were probably involved in this fighting, including Hasan Gina. The Ballista fell apart, and General Hoxha consolidated his power over the nation.

After the war, Hoxha aligned himself with Russia and later with China. He was paranoid and cruel. Any opposition, real or imagined, was eliminated. This included Shyti, who had risked his life to ferry the last three nurses to safety. Though he'd remained neutral, he was related to enemies of Hoxha and considered a threat. He spent many years under house arrest. Hoxha's opposition also included Kostig Steffa, who Hoxha felt was disloyal. He was tortured and killed.

· · · · ·

Because the people involved in the incredible story in Albania were forbidden from talking about it, the story nearly died. Agnes Jensen had taken careful notes, but her diary had been taken by American officials. Orville Abbott, too, had recorded notes – but somehow he'd kept them hidden from those who questioned him in Bari. The following year, Abbott turned his notes into a book-length memoir. He showed them to a reporter named Allen Field Smith. Smith helped him revise and type the book.

Abbott asked the army censors if he could publish it, and to his surprise – probably because he had obscured their actual route and hadn't named anyone who helped them – they gave him approval. But Abbott wasn't able to find a publisher willing to take it.

After the war, the escapees talked very little about their ordeal in Albania, even with their families. They mostly lost touch with one another as well. Hayes and Abbott wrote to each other for years. But it wasn't until 1983 that Harold Hayes organized a reunion for the 40th anniversary of their crash landing. When they got together in Columbus, Ohio, a reporter from the Associated Press showed up to record the event. Abbott had died by then, but many of the others made it. They swapped stories and looked at Jensen's scrapbook.

Abbott had worked for decades in a car factory. He'd put away his manuscript in a footlocker. He didn't talk much about the Albanian experience with his family, and he died in 1982. His story may have died with him if his son, Clint, hadn't learned about the book from his uncle George. Clint couldn't find the manuscript, but he was inspired to get in touch with Agnes Jensen, Harold

Hayes and other surviving members of the party. He began to research the story in earnest. Eventually he tracked down the daughter of Allen Smith, the reporter who had helped his dad with his manuscript. Marcia Smith was able to find a copy of Orville's manuscript among her father's things. Using his dad's manuscript as a core, Clint added information he had uncovered through his research and self-published *Out of Albania* in 2010.

· · · · ·

Hoxha's cruel rein as dictator of Albania was the biggest reason that Agnes Jensen waited so long to tell her story. She didn't want anyone who had helped the Americans to face danger from Hoxha. But Hoxha died in 1985, and a few years later Communism collapsed. Albania began to move towards becoming a democratic country.

In 1995, Jensen returned to Albania with a journalist and Albanian historian called Peter Lucas. They found the crash site. It showed no evidence of the old plane there. They also visited Dukat and Berat. In Berat, Jensen visited Steffa's widow, who told her what had happened to him. Jensen also learned that Hasan Gina had died in 1986. Because of Hasan's work helping the Allies, his father had been tortured by Ballists and died later from his injuries.

Jensen's return to Albania was emotional, but it was also inspiring. The military had returned her diary after the war was over. After her trip to Albania, she turned her notes into a memoir, published in 1999.

The story of the Americans trapped in Albania is a testament to the strength that people can find when they need to. It's also a testament to the basic goodness of humans. It took a huge network of individuals, many of whom put their lives on the line, to rescue the nurses, medics and flight crew who had been trapped behind enemy lines.

The nurses and medics of the 807th MAETS squadron were riding in a C-53 military transport plane like this when they crash-landed in the mountains of Albania.

Ten of the rescued nurses pose for the press at the hospital in Bari, Italy. From left to right they are: (front row) Gertrude "Tooie" Dawson, Elna Schwant, Lois Watson, Lillian Tacina, Ann Kopsco, (back row) Ann Markowitz, Frances Nelson, Agnes Jensen, Eugenie Rutkowski and Pauleen Kanable.

The medics and flight crew pose for the press during their stay at the hospital in Bari, Italy. From left to right: Gilbert Hornsby, Dick Lebo, Charles Adams, Robert Cranson, Willis Shumway, Paul Allen, William Eldridge, James Cruise, Robert Owen, Gordon MacKinnon, Raymond Ebers, Harold Hayes, Lawrence (Orville) Abbott, Charles Zeiber and John Wolf.

The flight crew: co-pilot James Baggs, pilot Charles Thrasher, radio operator Dick Lebo and crew chief Willis Shumway

Tooie Dawson reaches out her hand to greet her commanding officer upon arriving in Bari, Italy.

Medical military transport planes had bunks such as the ones shown to allow medical staff to care for wounded soldiers.

The nurses and medics beam with joy as their ship reaches the port in Bari, Italy.

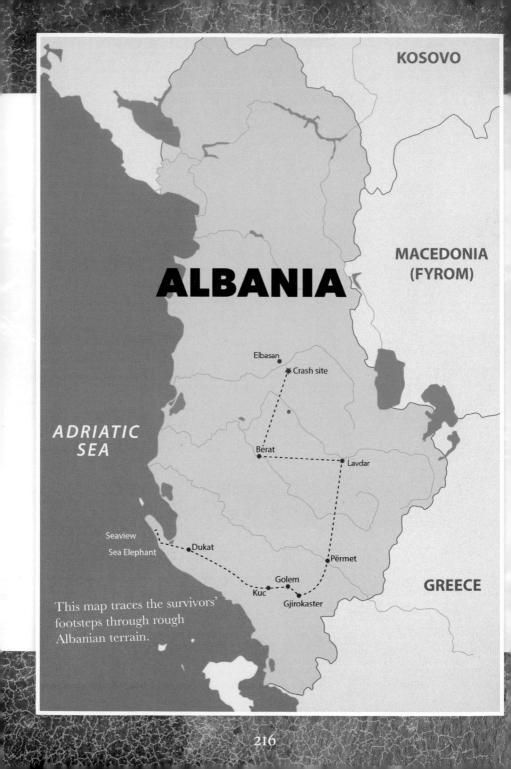

KOSOVO

MACEDONIA
(FYROM)

ALBANIA

ADRIATIC
SEA

Elbasan

☀ Crash site

Bërat

Lavdar

Seaview
Sea Elephant

Dukat

Përmet

GREECE

Golem

Kuc

Gjirokaster

This map traces the survivors'
footsteps through rough
Albanian terrain.

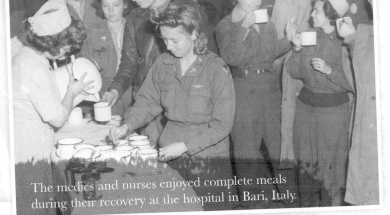

The medics and nurses enjoyed complete meals during their recovery at the hospital in Bari, Italy.

Some nurses of the 807th show off the men's shoes they were given when their own shoes fell apart.

TIMELINE

DECEMBER 1942:
Medical Air Evacuation Squadron (MAETS) is established.

8 NOVEMBER 1943:
The 807th MAETS crash-lands in Albania.

12 NOVEMBER 1943:
The Americans reach the city of Berat after a three-day walk.

15 NOVEMBER 1943:
The Nazis attack Berat; the Americans become split into three groups.

18 NOVEMBER 1943:
Two of the groups of Americans reunite in the hills of Albania;
three nurses remain stranded in a farmhouse in Berat.

19 NOVEMBER 1943:
The British forces in Albania are notified of the stranded Americans.

27 NOVEMBER 1943:
The Americans meet British Captain Victor Smith.

29 DECEMBER 1943:
The US-led aeroplane rescue attempt fails.

8 JANUARY 1944:
The Americans, minus the three stranded nurses in Berat, reach the Albanian
coast. There a rescue boat, *The Yankee*, meets them.

9 JANUARY 1944:
The rescue boat reaches Bari, Italy.

21 MARCH 1944:
The remaining three nurses reach the Albanian coast, where a rescue boat
transports them to Bari, Italy.

QUOTATION SOURCE NOTES

Albanian Escape: The True Story of U.S. Army Nurses Behind Enemy Lines, Agnes Jensen Mangerich (University Press of Kentucky, 2006) pages: 16, 28(2,3), 74, 80, 90, 94, 99, 100, 107(2,4), 156(1)

Out of Albania: A True Account of a WWII Underground Rescue Mission, Lawrence O. Abbot and Clinton W. Abbott (LuLu Press, 2010) pages: 8, 33–36, 41, 70, 72–73, 87(1), 96, 101–105, 155, 162, 166, 172, 175

Savage Will: The Daring Escape of Americans Trapped Behind Nazi Lines, Timothy M. Gay (Penguin Group, 2013) pages: 9, 28(1), 30, 48, 87(2), 107(1,3,5), 145, 156(2), 184

The Secret Rescue: An Untold Story of American Nurses and Medics Behind Nazi Lines, Cate Lineberry (Back Bay Books/Little, Brown and Company, 2014) pages: 56, 111, 114, 124, 144, 165, 186

ABOUT THE AUTHOR

Eric Braun writes fiction and non-fiction for children, teenagers and adults, but sometimes he still dreams of being a professional skateboarder. He lives in Minneapolis, USA, with his wife, sons, dog and gecko.

GLOSSARY

anti-aircraft describes weapons designed to defend against attacks from the air

apprehension state of being worried and slightly afraid

artillery cannons and other large guns used during battles

Axis group of countries that fought together in World War II; the Axis powers included Japan, Italy and Germany

bandolier belt worn over the shoulder and across the chest, often with pockets used to carry items

casualty someone who is injured, captured, killed or missing in an accident, a disaster or a war

censor person whose duty it is to remove material an organization considers objectionable

clandestine conducted with secrecy

classified top secret

confiscate take something away from someone as a punishment or because that thing is not allowed

dysentery serious infection of the intestines that can be deadly; dysentery is often caused by drinking contaminated water

execute put a person to death as punishment for a crime

fascist form of government ruled by a dictator that promotes extreme nationalism, repression, and anti-communism

fuselage main body of an aeroplane

guerilla warfare using small surprise attacks rather than large battles

insignia badge or design that shows someone's rank or membership in an organization

insulated covered with a material that stops heat from escaping

medic soldier trained to give medical help in an emergency or during a battle

memoir narrative work composed from personal experience

militia group of volunteer citizens who serve as soldiers in emergencies

morphine opium-based drug often used as a painkiller

Nazi political party led by Adolf Hitler; the Nazis ruled Germany from 1933 to 1945

obscure make it difficult to see something

pneumonia serious disease that causes the lungs to become inflamed and filled with a thick fluid that makes breathing difficult

propaganda information that is spread to influence the way people think, gain supporters or damage an opposing group; propaganda is often incomplete or biased information

strafe heavily attack those on the ground with machine gun fire from close range

telegram message that is sent by telegraph

unsanitary unclean

BOOKS

Courage & Defiance: Stories of Spies, Saboteurs, and Survivors in World War II Denmark, Deborah Hopkinson (Scholastic Press, 2015)

Pilots in Peril!: The Untold Story of U.S. Pilots Who Braved "the Hump" in World War II, Steven Otfinoski (Capstone Press, 2016)

Resisting the Nazis (Heroes of World War II), Claire Throp (Raintree, 2015)

Women Heroes of World War II: 26 Stories of Espionage, Sabotage, Resistance, and Rescue, Kathryn J. Atwood (Chicago Review Press, 2011)

COMPREHENSION QUESTIONS

1. Why did the Americans end up walking nearly 1,609 kilometres when they crashed only about 97 kilometres from Seaview?

2. The Americans were helped by several Albanians, including Hasan Gina, Kostig Steffa and Quani Siqueca (Johnny). Compare and contrast two of them.

3. How did Orville Abbott's life before the war affect his point of view about his time in Albania?

SELECT BIBLIOGRAPHY

Albanian Escape, Agnes Jensen (University of Kentucky Press, 1999)

Out of Albania, Lawrence O. Abbott and Clinton W. Abbott (LuLu Press, 2010)

"Q&A: Last Survivor of a Dramatic WW2 Rescue", Cate Lineberry (National Geographic, 2013)

Savage Will, Timothy M. Gay (NAL Caliber, 2013)

The Secret Rescue, Cate Lineberry (Little, Brown, 2013)

WEBSITES

www.bbc.com/news/world-europe-guernsey-34176824

In 2015, a memorial was erected on Guernsey, one of the Channel Islands, to commemorate Allied aircrew who died around Guernsey.

www.iwm.org.uk/history/the-secret-british-organisation-of-the-second-world-war

Find out more about the Special Operations Executive (SOE) and World War II in general on the Imperial War Museum's website.

INDEX